PRAISE FOR L.Y. MARLOW

Color Me Butterfly

"With a clear and courageous voice, L.Y. Marlow reveals the unspeakable horrors of a family's legacy. After four generations of women and children are held captive within a dark chrysalis of domestic violence, one of them finds the strength to break free. Color Me Butterfly is a haunting journey that ultimately leads towards miraculous healing and renewed spirit."

—Beth Hoffman,
bestselling author of *Saving CeeCee Honeycutt*

"Based on the author's own horrifying true tale of four generations of women surviving domestic abuse, Butterfly powerfully illuminates the emotional impact of a crime that claims the lives of more than three women a day."

—*Essence*

A Life Apart

"A forbidden interracial attraction spans decades of secret involvement and some surprising attachments to reach a place of forgiveness. In her second book, Marlow displays an emotional sensitivity that lends heart to her story. The passing of the years brings shocks, achievements and unexpected late reconciliation. Marlow deftly tugs the heartstrings throughout."

—*Kirkus Reviews*

DON'T LOOK

AT THE

MONSTER

DON'T LOOK
AT THE
MONSTER

One Woman's Journey to Embrace a Purposeful Life

the Gifts, the Lessons, the Blessings

L. Y. MARLOW

Published in the United States by L.Y. Marlow Productions.

Distributed by Ingram.
For ordering information or special discounts, please contact Ingram.

Library of Congress Cataloging-in-Publication Data

Marlow, L. Y. (Lydia Y.)
Don't Look at the Monster:
One Woman's Journey to Embrace a Purposeful Life / L. Y. Marlow — 1st ed.
p. cm.
1. Marlow, L.Y. (Lydia Y.)—Authors, American—21st century—Biography. 2. Auto-biography. 3. Self-Help—Motivational—Inspirational. I. Title.

ISBN: 978-0-692-83017-8
eBook ISBN: 978-0-692-77579-0

Jacket and book design by Kim Hall Design
Jacket photograph: Bigstock

Printed in the United States of America

First Edition

For Ma—
who gave me the courage
to face my monsters

CONTENTS

PART 1: THE GIFTS

PART 2: THE LESSONS

PART 3: THE BLESSINGS

AUTHOR'S NOTE

To write this book, I relied on my personal journals, research, and memories of the stories and events as I recalled them. To protect identities, I occasionally changed the names of most, but not all, individuals that appear in the book, and in some cases, I also modified certain identifying details to preserve anonymity. All events described herein actually happened, although I may have omitted some people and events, but only if that event or person had no impact on the substance of the story.

PROLOGUE

The first time I met a *real* monster, I was eight years old.

It was the summer of 1975, and Ma let me go to New York City to spend the whole summer with Aunt Deller, Uncle Ralph, and their children, Denise and Leonard. At fourteen and eleven, they were much bigger than me, already had life tucked up under their chins.

Leonard was a mischievous little bastard. In less than a week, he had found ways to scare the little Jesus out of me. That weekend when Aunt Deller and Uncle Ralph took us to Coney Island in Brooklyn, Leonard had convinced them to let us see a vintage show. I thought nothing of it as I stood at the front of the crowd packed inside a makeshift tent. A big blue cotton candy in one hand, a rainbow snow cone in the other, my eyes glued to the brunette who sat in a bikini in the middle of a steel cage.

She was so beautiful, I hardly noticed Leonard standing closely behind me, snickering at the way I watched her. The way her café con leche skin, lustrous hair, and green eyes, even in the dimmed light, seemed to shimmer. I imagined how I could look if only my pigtails would behave. I smiled and was convinced she smiled back at me too.

Suddenly the room became pitch dark; the crowd hushed to a silence as a spotlight centered on her. Then, slowly, deliberately, coarse black hair started to grow on her, everywhere! From the top of her head down to the tips of her toes. Then she got bigger and bigger and bigger until gradually she transformed into a gorilla.

I shot out of there! Ran so fast, I nearly crapped my pants.

Aunt Deller, Uncle Ralph, Denise, and even Leonard trailed closely behind, trying to catch me.

But nothing could stop me. I wanted to get as far away from that thing as I could get. I jetted past the Ferris wheel, the merry-go-round, my scrawny legs defying gravity before I went colliding into a concrete wall, a rusty nail protruding from it.

Blood was everywhere!

Aunt Deller nearly fainted when she finally caught up to me. "Girl, why the hell you go running like that for? Now look at you!"

It took a slew of stitches and some more tongue-lashing from Aunt Deller to seal the gash in my head. A scar that stuck with me for years to come.

Have you ever encountered something that scared you so terribly that it made you flee, forced you to run until you hit a concrete wall, or stopped you dead in your tracks?

Monsters were what I would come to label them.

My monsters showed up decades later when I was faced with some of the most difficult and terrifying moments of my life. It would take some wise words from my three-year-old granddaughter, Promise, when I called her late one evening drowning in my tears. *Just close your eyes real tight and just don't look at the monster*, she had said to me. The same as I'd once told her when she discovered she was afraid of the dark. Now, those words would ultimately change my life.

PART 1

THE GIFTS

"Monsters are real, and ghosts are real too.
They live inside us, and sometimes, they win."
—Stephen King

It's Terrifying

Have you ever encountered something that was so terrifying that you questioned if things could get any worse? Ironically, the moments that frighten us the most are also the ones that strengthen us. But instead of embracing it, we allow life's demons—our monsters—to get in the way. Make no bones about it, monsters are very much real. But know this . . . confronting our monsters helps us to face our fears, uncover who we really are, and unlock the possibilities of who we are to become.

I HATE NANCY

No matter how many empowerment books you read or positive thoughts you try to feed your soul, every now and again, there will come a time when you are faced with something or someone you will come to loathe, and your faith, your resolve, is tested. My someone, my something, was Nancy.

One cold afternoon in December 2009, we had arrived in Houston. Me, Ma, John, and Nancy.

I hardly slept through the first night, just lay there, listening to Nancy snore. Ma and John lay in the bed across from mine. My head felt clouded, my body fatigued. I hadn't slept much in weeks.

It was still dark when I heard Ma stir, slowly sitting up on the edge of the bed. I turned to face her, watched her silhouette in the morning dawn. I knew her habits now, had come to know them these past eight weeks.

She sat on the edge of her bed, the mask nearly covering her face, her thoughts a twisted tangle of fate. Then, haltingly, she mustered enough strength to stand and drag her much thinner frame into the bathroom.

I lay still, listening to the running water, the hacking cough, her measured breaths.

The cough was worse than it was the day before, and the day before that. Every morning it got worse. I looked over at Nancy, rolled my eyes.

I could hear her labored breaths, then the coughing again. I rushed to the door, knocked. "Ma, are you okay?"

She didn't say anything. I leaned in closer. "Ma?"

"I'm fine."

I sat back on the bed, looked over at John, at the sadness on his face. So different from his face just three months ago, on our last family vacation.

It was our last day aboard the carnival cruise ship, the morning of the Captain's Dinner when I awoke with a persistent and urgent thought. I didn't understand it. I just knew we *had* to do it.

I quickly dressed and rushed to the gift shop.

A middle-aged woman in a floral smock and plain skirt was hanging more photos on a wall full of hundreds of photos of people taken that week.

"I'd like to make a reservation to take a family photo this evening,"

"This evening? I think we're all booked."

"But we gotta do it tonight. We leave tomorrow."

She pulled the appointment book from under the counter and scanned it. "No, I'm sorry, we're all booked being it's Captain's Night. We don't have nothing available until ten p.m."

"But that's too late. It has to be before dinner when we'll all be together."

She looked at me, annoyed.

"Please. Can you squeeze us in? Please!"

She looked down at the book again. I waited.

"Well . . . if y'all could be there at seven fifteen, I'll ask the photographer to squeeze you in."

"We'll be there! Thank you!"

"You're gonna have to be on time; otherwise, he'll cancel your appointment."

"We won't be late."

I hurried to the upper deck, spotted Ma lying on a lounge chair in a navy blue bathing suit, a wide sun hat, and sunglasses, looking out at an eternity of bluish-green ocean. My stepfather, John, lay next to her in khaki shorts and a plaid short-sleeved shirt, reading a paper.

I rushed over to them. "I made a reservation for us to take a family photo at seven fifteen this evening."

"What are you talking about? We've taken plenty of pictures already."

"I know. But we don't have a family portrait of all of us together. You, John, and us kids."

Ma stared at me, puzzled. "Alright then. If you can get everyone together, that's fine with me."

I quickly made my way around the ship to look for Eileen, Roy Jr., and Anthony. There were five of us, all now in our mid- to late forties. Roy Jr. was the eldest, then Eileen, followed by Anthony, then me, now the youngest, after our youngest sister, Angie, passed away twenty years earlier.

We had always been close, spending nearly every holiday, birthdays, and annual vacations with Ma. Christmas was our favorite time of the year. Not only because of the gifts and toys that Ma saved up all year to buy for us kids, but because of how we would pool our lunch allowances and money we earned from odd jobs to buy Ma and John and the rest of the family the best gifts we could afford. Every Christmas, Roy Jr., being the eldest, would organize us—our budget, how much we would spend for each gift, and who would be responsible for getting what. Around mid-November, he would sit us down in his room and tell us, *Make sure y'all start saving up your lunch money from now on.* Then he'd collect the money and hold it in a safe place until it was time to shop. We loved shopping for Ma, paying attention all year to the small things she went without and the things she'd like. On Christmas morning, we would be as excited to see her open her gifts as much as we were about opening the gifts she got for us. *Y'all kids don't need to be spending all that money on me,* Ma would tell us. But we never listened. It was the only way we knew how to give her back as much as she'd sacrificed for us.

Now, when I finally found Eileen, Roy Jr., and Anthony, I said, "We have reservations to take a family photo with Ma and John at seven fifteen this evening before dinner. Don't be late!"

They all gave me a peculiar look, but showed up on time. Ready.

Ma wore a chiffon cream and black dress, draped off her shoulders, her hair perfectly styled. John's dark suit and light blue shirt and tie complemented her. They looked so beautiful. Eileen wore a black dress and Anthony and Roy Jr. wore dark suits. I stuck out like a sore thumb in my orange blouse and floral skirt because no one told me that Captain's Night was formal. It was my first cruise, and I wasn't even supposed to be there, but Ma made me go, told me it may be her last family vacation because she'd be retiring at the end of the year. So I went to the doctor, stocked up on some motion sickness meds, and set sail.

The Family Photo the Night of the Captain's Dinner. From L to R:
Anthony, me, Roy Jr., Eileen, John, and Ma in the middle.
To view, visit: lymarlow.com/images

A few days after we returned from the cruise, I called Ma.

"You don't sound so good. Did you catch a cold on the ship?"

"I'm not sure. I can't seem to catch my breath. I ain't never had no asthma or nothin'."

"Sounds like you may have caught something. Maybe you should go to the doctor."

Within a few weeks, me, Ma, John, Promise, and Nancy sat quietly in a sterile white room. Ma, on the exam table with John in the seat across from her, and me, Promise, and Nancy in the corner.

I stared at Ma then over at John, watched him watching her.

She sat on the exam table covered by a thin sheet of white paper in a cotton smock that tied at her back, her hands locked together in her lap, her face down.

This was the third time we'd sat in somebody's sterile white room with Ma sitting on the table watching her hands, waiting. Other than an occasional cold and the leg that ached when the weather was bad, Ma had been fine a few short weeks ago, just fine. What did those doctors know anyway? They had no idea who Ma was. And how could they expect some skimpy test to suddenly dictate Ma's life? They were *wrong*. Dead *wrong*. Just WRONG.

I watched Promise, her curious two-year-old mind fixated on the objects on the desk that became her toys before we heard a tap on the door. I sat up straight when the doctor walked in. Dr. Bhat was short and stout with almond-colored skin and salt-and-pepper hair. He wore dark slacks and a white lab coat over a shirt and tie. I could tell he was the serious type. He took a seat at the desk with his clipboard and gave us a half-hearted smile, glanced over at Nancy and then looked straight at Ma.

"I took a look at your X-rays, scans, and lab work. The tests are conclusive. It's Stage IV lung cancer."

I gasped, went still as though I had not heard those words before, as though my heart was not already broken.

"With this type of cancer, it spreads rapidly."

"What do you mean spread rapidly?" My lips were quivering now.

He consulted his notes again, then looked back up at me. "From what we can see so far, it's metastatic, meaning the cancer is in both lungs, her lymph nodes, and it may have already spread to other parts of her organs, including her brain."

Tears streamed down my face, under my chin, onto my clothes. I thought I'd prepared myself for this, told myself that no matter what this doctor said, even if he said the same thing that the other two doctors had told us, no matter what, I'd be prepared. Ma was only sixty-five, and I couldn't bear the thought of living without her.

I wiped my face and looked straight at him again, trying desperately to compose myself. "What are our options?"

He glanced at his notes. "Well, the cancer is progressing rapidly. It's too far along to do much else except try to slow it down with radiation and chemo. She could have possibly six months, maybe a little longer with the treatments. There's not much else we can do."

"What do you mean there's not much else you can do? You just said that like you're not even going to try!"

"Lydia!"

"No, Ma! He's just sitting there talking to us like he don't care." I couldn't control what I was saying, let alone the tears that streamed down my face. I wanted to argue away what he said, as though my anger could defeat the cancer.

"Look, my job is to tell you the prognosis. As much as I wish there was more we can do, I can't make any promises. We care for a lot of patients like this, and we can't go around giving them false hope."

"False hope? How dare you!"

"Lydia! Stop it!"

"No, Ma! He can't talk to us like that. He's got no right to take our hope away!"

"Lydia, he's only doing his job," John spoke up.

"His job is to help Ma get better! Not sit there talking to us like he's already given up on her!"

"Look, I know this is very difficult for you and your family. Trust me, if I could have better news or do something different, I would."

I looked over at Ma, tears streaming down my face.

She held my eyes. Just held them. "It's fine. It's in God's hands."

Waves of emotions pulsed through me. My heart was pounding, my legs were shaking, and I felt sick. I opened my mouth to say something, but nothing else came out.

"I'd like you to start the chemo and radiation treatments right away. I'm going to send the nurse in to schedule it. Do you have any more questions for me?"

I wiped my face, closed my eyes for a moment and just sat there, not caring that he was watching me. I finally took a breath, opened my eyes, and looked square at him. "The only question I have for you is who do I talk to get my mother's records?"

He held my stare, then grabbed the file and patted Ma on the knee before he left.

A few minutes later the nurse walked in. "I understand you'd like to release your mother's records?"

"Yes, and I'd also like to file a complaint."

She took a seat at the desk, reached over, and grabbed my hand, held it. "Look, I know this isn't easy. But we are a good hospital with one of the best cancer treatment centers. Let me send one of the other doctors in to talk to you before you take your mother somewhere else. I know this must be really hard, but maybe one of the other doctors can help better explain things. Would that help?"

I looked over again at Ma, watched her nod.

"Yes."

This time the doctor who came in looked to be in her mid-forties, with short brown hair and kind eyes. First, she told us that she was an oncologist specializing in lung cancer. Then she helped us to understand the type of cancer Ma had, small cell lung cancer, which spreads quickly. "I consulted her lab tests, X-rays, and scans, and the results do show signs that the cancer has metastasized. That is why we have to treat it very aggressively. Let me show you." She pulled one of the X-rays from an oversized file that she brought in with her, and posted it up on a small X-ray reader that hung on the wall above Nancy. "See here," she pointed to the X-ray. "This is where we can see that the cancer has spread. Fortunately, from what I can tell, it's localized to small areas so far, which means we may be able to contain it. But we need to begin a treatment plan immediately."

"What are her chances of beating this if we agree to the treatments?" I could hear my own voice inside my head, a distant whisper.

She consulted the file again, glanced over at John, then at Ma and me. "While the prognosis for this type of cancer at this stage is very grave, I have treated similar patients whose cancer has gone into remission. It's difficult to say because there are so many factors involved. First, we need to see how well your mother responds to the chemo. We may have to try a few to see which is most effective for her. Then the radiation treatments will help to shrink the tumors. We also need to put her on a nutritional plan and other therapies to boost her immune system. Everything will help. But we need for you to keep a good spirit," she said, looking over again at Ma. "I imagine that this must be very difficult for you, and we're going to do everything we can to beat this." She smiled at Ma, and Ma smiled back.

After she left, the nurse came back in and scheduled appointments for Ma's treatment to start. When she was done, she handed us a card with instructions to call anytime if we had questions or just wanted to talk.

We were all exhausted by the time we left. Part of me was feeling better and part of me was still confused, angry. Though we knew little more than we did hours ago when we first arrived, this time we were leaving with something we so desperately needed, something that lightened my heart and made Ma smile for the first time in weeks—*hope.*

That was the first of countless doctor visits watching Ma lie on a table, week after dreadful week, radiation beamed into her frail body, and clear liquid dripped from a bag into her veins—chemo—stripping her of every ounce of energy, hair, and dignity, and making her so sick that she had to be hospitalized three times. I'd sleep in the chair next to Ma's bed, and when she was released, I'd lie outside her bedroom door on the living room floor of the small apartment that she and John rented after they sold their home. At the end of the year when Ma retired, they were planning to move into the retirement home they'd purchased in Lugoff, a small Southern town near Columbia, South Carolina.

I'd lie on that floor, listening to Nancy's snarls and Ma screaming in agony through the night, the pain so unbearable, praying to God to heal her. I, unlike Ma, was *angry* with God. I didn't understand how He could let this happen to her. With all the miserable people in the world, what did Ma do to deserve this? Ma worshipped Him. Prayed every day. Went to church every Sunday. Paid her tithes. Short of a few cuss words once, maybe twice, a year when she'd get so frustrated at something or somebody that she'd let one go and then repent, Ma was a good

Christian woman, a noble wife, and the best mama. She took care of her family, us kids, in ways that I still did not understand. She'd been through so much already, having survived torturous abuse most of her young life at the hands of her father, only to later marry my father, who beat her worse than her own daddy had. Then as though that wasn't difficult enough, she watched the man, my father—who had viciously beaten her most of their married life—be violently stabbed in front of her by two white men because of the color of his skin, leaving her a widow to care for five small children. Years later, Ma would bury her youngest child, who committed suicide by jumping in front of a train at the tender age of eighteen; then she had to take care of her ailing mother, who died of lung cancer. Hadn't Ma endured enough?

Why Ma, God? Why?

Now, I sat on a queen bed in a Hilton Hotel room in Houston, wondering how until twelve weeks ago, Ma could be so seemingly healthy: No sickness. No symptoms. No nothing. One day Ma was sitting at the head of the family table smiling, then suddenly, it was like someone took the Etch A Sketch of our lives, turned our family upside down, and shook it and shook it and shook it.

After a while, I decided that if conventional medicines weren't going to save Ma, then I had to do it. As a little girl, I used to fantasize about being Wonder Woman, telling myself all I had to do was twirl around to change from a scrawny little thing who was afraid of her own shadow into a superhero who could use her lasso and purple rays to do or be or save anyone. Nearly forty years later, the fantasy was gone, replaced by a façade that threatened to crack.

I was going to save Ma.

Finally, Ma came out of the bathroom and took a seat on the bed to catch her breath. John and I waited to see if she needed anything. I'd already laid her clothes out on the bed.

After a few minutes, I went into the bathroom and put away the towels and toiletries she'd left behind. It took me no time to brush my teeth, shower, and dress before I was standing at the makeshift kitchen fixing Ma's breakfast—whole grain petite bagels, Smucker's sugar free jam (everything had to be sugar free because cancer thrives on sugar), grapefruit, and water. I ate too though it was too early for me, but I wanted to share that moment with her.

By eight forty-five, we were in the car headed to the Burzynski Clinic, an innovative cancer treatment center I'd learned about when I saw Suzanne Somers appear on a morning show to discuss her new book, *Knockout*. Dr. Burzynski was one of the doctors that she said was curing cancer. I devoured the book, contacted the center, sent them all of Ma's records, and begged them to take her. Within a few weeks, I packed up Ma, and we moved into a Hilton Hotel in Houston, near the clinic.

The center was only six miles away, but we left forty-five minutes early so as not to be late. *We could not* be late.

When we walked into the center, we were greeted by a very friendly woman who gave us a sheet of paper with Ma's name already printed on it and an itinerary of appointments.

I quickly handed over an oversized orange expandable folder with all of Ma's medical records, test results, and everything else I'd collected from every doctor, hospital, clinic, and healthcare professional from the moment Ma was diagnosed.

It took them no time to lead me, John, Ma, and Nancy back to an exam room, identical to the rooms that we'd been in lately, except it seemed *different*.

The doctor who finally came in was young, but from the moment he opened his mouth, I was confident he knew what he was talking about. He told us about the clinic and what to expect, then meticulously went through a series of questions, covering every detail about Ma's medical history, recent diagnosis, and treatment plans. I often consulted my yellow spiral notebook—*my bible*—full of my own personal notes detailing every diagnosis, treatment, nutritional plan, and insurance information, words I'd not once thought about until now: *Cancer. Stage IV. Metastasize. Malignant. Radiation. Taxol/Carbo* (one of many chemotherapy drugs). Everything I needed to know to help them help Ma.

"Since our approach includes a treatment called antineoplaston therapy, which targets cancer cells without harming the good cells, we need to do some more tests and bloodwork so we can tailor your treatment. How well you respond to the treatment will determine the extent and duration of your treatment. It could take weeks. It could take months. We're not sure until we see how you respond. Some patients respond very quickly. Others take longer. You'll come to the center daily for your treatments, and we'll monitor how well you're responding. Does that make sense?"

I looked over at Ma. I could tell from the look on her face that she was tired.

"Yes, we understand." I spoke up for Ma. The same way I'd been speaking up since the moment that horrid six-letter word crept into our lives and tried to steal Ma away. Quite frankly, he could have been speaking *Klingon* for all I cared. As long as they were going to save Ma.

"Alright then. I'll send the nurse in to get your bloodwork. Then she'll arrange for a PET scan and for you to be seen by other members of our team. Once all the test results are back in a few days, we will start your treatment."

By midday, we were back in the lounge waiting for Ma to be seen by another doctor when in walked Suzanne Somers. She was there to shoot a documentary.

She still reminded me of Chrissy from *Three's Company* except she was more poised, more mature, and surrounded by a team of people, including Dr. Burzynski.

"That's Suzanne Somers."

Ma turned and looked at her, but she was so exhausted, I don't think it registered.

"You know. The celebrity I told you about. The one who wrote the book about doctors that are curing cancer and Dr. Burzynski and this clinic."

"That's her right there?" John gestured toward the group.

"Yeah, that's her."

Before I knew it, I was making my way over to her.

"Hello. My name is L.Y. Marlow and I wanted to let you know that you inspired me to bring my mother here. I can't believe you're here now! What a coincidence."

I told Suzanne everything. About Ma being diagnosed eight weeks ago. About how the other doctors had given up on Ma, and her book was the reason we were there. I don't know why I said something about the generations of women in my family, including Ma, that had been abused, but for some reason it all made sense at the time. Maybe I thought cancer was another form of abuse.

"What type of cancer does your mother have?"

"Stage IV lung cancer." For the first time in weeks, I was able to say those words without becoming unstitched.

She reached over and hugged me, and when she let go, she said, "Nothing is ever a coincidence."

PEPTO-BISMOL

I was three-and-a-half years old when I had my first dose of Pepto-Bismol, the day I reached to grab a hot frying pan from the stove. Though the scar would take years to fade, the scare would stay with me forever.

Ma waited for John to hand her the needle that she stuck in her belly twice a day, and the first of eight pills she would down with water. She hadn't yet removed the wig that hovered over her bald head or the glasses that shielded her blank eyes.

I watched her pierce her flesh with the needle, and then I rushed into the bathroom, closed the door behind me, and cried. Slow waves of muffled sobs, my hands heavy on the vanity, holding me up. I looked in the mirror at my face, my eyes, deep with dark circles. I looked tired, frail like Ma.

I splashed cold water on my face then wiped it and the sink, everything, before I heard a tap on the door and opened it to find Ma, John, and Nancy waiting for me.

"We better get going before we're late for our appointment. I'm going to bring the car up to the front entrance."

I rushed to get everything—my *bible*, Ma's purse, Nancy. Then I held open Ma's jacket, watched her delicately ease her way into it, the long cord hanging from her nostrils. We walked slowly down the hall and through the hotel lobby where we were greeted by the lady behind the check-in desk, the concierge, and the man cleaning the lobby. They had all come to know us.

When we stepped outside the hotel, John hurried to help Ma into the car as I climbed into the backseat. We rode in silence, except for Nancy and the busy freeway noise that wafted through the open window. I stared out the window at the drifting landscape. It all looked familiar to me now.

We arrived at the clinic early and had been there only a few minutes when a tall, thin woman with curly blond hair approached me.

"There's a problem with your mother's insurance. We need to go and see the insurance coordinator."

I was annoyed because I didn't want to miss Ma's first treatment. I followed her to the administrative office where I was greeted by a soft-spoken African-American woman who introduced herself as Linda.

"Your mother's insurance will not pay for the PET scan. Can you call them?"

I referred to my *bible* and found Ma's insurance information. I knew exactly who to call because I had already made countless calls to get Ma's Medicare, disability, and social security benefits, which amounted to a lousy $700 a month!

Ma had worked hard all of her life to keep us kids fed, clothed, and a roof over our heads. Now that she needed the insurance she had worked so hard to earn, the insurance company refused to approve her PET scan.

The insurance company wasn't there when Ma's beautiful caramel face and her scarred, bald head turned ash gray from the high doses of radiation that penetrated her skull. The insurance company wasn't there to hear Ma scream through the night. The insurance company wasn't there when a nurse told me to gather the family because Ma wouldn't make it.

The insurance company wasn't there then, and the insurance company wasn't there now!

I was livid by the time I heard a voice on the other end of the line. "I want to speak with your supervisor!"

I heard a click, silence, then a recorded message that rambled on forever.

Linda motioned to a chair, and I sat down and noticed the piles of papers and the family photos on her desk.

Waiting gave me time to think—about all the times I was too busy doing *nothing* to visit Ma; about the calls I missed, the holidays I skipped, the excuses I gave; about all the things I wished were different.

I didn't realize I was crying again until Linda reached over to hand me a tissue.

"I imagine this must be very hard for you. What type of cancer does your mother have?"

I wiped the tears. "Lung cancer."

"Well, I'm gonna pray for her."

I looked back down at my bible. I didn't want to talk anymore. I was tired of talking. Tired of arguing. Tired of praying.

The lady who finally came on the other end of the line was much more understanding than the people who refused to approve Ma's PET scan. She approved it, and I quickly made my way back to find Ma, John, and Nancy waiting for me.

Ma met my eyes. "I saw the nutritionist and the doctor should be calling us in soon."

I nodded at Ma, then lay back and closed my eyes to relieve the tension in my head. When I opened them again, there was a man sitting across from us slumped in a wheelchair with a blanket over him. His face was gaunt with dark, lifeless eyes and thinning hair, and a woman sat next to him. I watched her, the way she gently adjusted the blanket, the way she touched his hand. I could tell that she was tired too.

I felt embarrassed when she caught me staring. Our eyes locked, and for a brief moment, we connected. It wasn't until I saw John stand to help Ma that I realized the nurse had called us.

I grabbed Ma's things and Nancy, and followed John, Ma, and the nurse back to the same room we had been in the day before.

We took the same seats and did what we had come to do every time we were escorted to one of those rooms. We didn't talk. We didn't move. We waited, each of us concealed in our own grief.

When the doctor finally came in, gave us the rundown again, and asked if we had any questions, we all shook our heads no.

"Alright then. I'll send the nurse in to administer the first treatment."

A few minutes later, the nurse showed up with two bottles with thick pink liquid inside that looked like Pepto-Bismol.

Our eyes were glued to the nurse as she poured a capsize full of the *Pepto-Bismol* into a small paper cup and handed it to Ma.

Ma sniffed it, then quickly gulp it down. My mind flooded with memories of all the times that Ma gave us kids Pepto-Bismol—when Roy Jr. would sneak in the pantry and eat spoonfuls of peanut butter that caused him to have diarrhea for a week; when Eileen got her period and said the cramps made her feel like she wanted to throw up; when Anthony got the measles and Ma said that the Pepto-Bismol would make the fever, the rash, and the runny nose all go away; when I, at age three, reached up and pulled a pot full of hot grease off the stove, and Ma gave it to me to ease the third-degree burns on my hand and arm; and when she would rub it on baby Angie's gums when she was teething.

If Ma thought Pepto-Bismol could fix anything, then doggone it, maybe Pepto-Bismol could cure cancer.

SUNDAY MORNINGS

There comes a time when life will stare you down, and every-thing, every miniscule thing you thought was important, will dim in comparison to what really matters, and it will all be reduced to that very moment.

She sat in the chair across from me reading a book I'd given her long ago. She looked so beautiful—her lovely caramel face framed by her delicate, bald head, her readers perched perfectly on her nose.

She looked the way I remembered her years ago: *flawless, soft, open,* and I was reminded of a time when I was seven years old. It was a Sunday morning. The house was quiet, lighted only by the sun that seeped through the draped windows. Barefoot, I'd tiptoed down two flights of stairs careful not to wake the other kids. Ma was sitting in the living room in her nightdress, oblivious, as she thought about the same things she thought about every Sunday morning: *What to cook with the grits for breakfast. What each child would wear to church. What to make for Sunday dinner.*

I sat at the bottom of the stairs, watching the peace on her face, and musing over how she could be so still. So very still.

At seven, my mind was always spinning. Always thinking. Just wouldn't shut up. Relief came only while gazing at Ma in the quiet of the ripe Sunday morning, the sanctuary that everything was going to be alright despite the Frigidaire that went kaput and caused a month's worth of food to spoil; the aches in her legs that she'd wrap so tight they swelled; and the small social security check, barely enough to pay the rent on the public housing, feed, and clothe five children, or make a house into a home.

Then with her eyes closed, she'd start to hum, the hymn buried beneath the sweet melody of her sound:

Why should I feel discouraged, why should the shadows come,
Why should my heart feel lonely, and long for heav'n and home,
When Jesus is my portion? My constant friend is He;
His eye is on the sparrow, and I know He watches me;
His eye is on the sparrow, and I know He watches me.
I sing because I'm happy, I sing because I'm free,
For His eye is on the sparrow, and I know He watches me.

I'd linger in Ma's shadow, and all the strife in my seven-year-old life would just plain vanish into thin air. Now I looked at her and thought about the first time I had noticed Ma's bald head. For some reason, I had dismissed the whole thing. Like I left home one day, and when I returned, Ma's hair was gone. And though her face was bloated, her skin pale from the acute anemia, both hands terribly bruised from the countless IVs, and patches of dark spots scarred her head from the high doses of radiation to kill off the cancer cells that had spread to her brain, there was something beautiful about her bald head.

Never in my life had I felt so lost. I had done all I knew how to do to defeat that wormy disease disguised in a six-letter word. I had traveled near and far, and made the acquaintance of every doctor, hospital, or clinic that I thought could cure Ma. I had prayed and tussled with God, then repented. And other than putting on some boxing gloves and jumping inside Ma's little, frail body to whoop *cancer's* ass, I didn't know what else I could do.

So I just looked at her with sheer pain in my heart. I *looked* at her.

"How do you like the book?" I finally managed to utter.

Ma glanced up at me, tried to smile. "It's a good story. I really like it."

"That was one of the books I read when I wrote *Color Me Butterfly*. It really inspired me."

Ma got a pensive look on her face. I could tell that she was thinking about *Cane River*—the story of four generations of slave women.

"I really like your book too."

I held her eyes because I knew exactly what she meant; she didn't have to say it: *Cane River* reminded her of our own story—four generations of abused women. Aside from watching Ma be so sick, that was one of the hardest things I had ever had to do—to write that book and relive the terrible stories of my grandmother, my mother, myself, and my daughter. The way my grandfather had brutalized my grandmother and her eight children—including Ma. And how Ma later met and married my father, who'd beaten her more viciously than Granddaddy had. Worse than writing about my grandmother and Ma's pain was reliving my own. It was an experience that tore back layers of hurt that I'd worked so hard to heal, only to have to peel more layers when my daughter became the fourth generation.

I felt the tears welling again. "Well, I better make your lunch. We'll need to leave soon for the clinic."

I rushed into the bathroom and closed the door behind me. I had never cried so much in my life. One minute, there I was talking to Ma, taking care of her; then the next minute, I'd break into pieces like fragile china. I couldn't stop thinking about all the things we did together as a family: The vacations. The Sunday dinners. The family gatherings. The way Ma used to take us kids to the park and we'd throw hot dogs and burgers on the grill, and then play kickball, Ma awkwardly kicking the ball, then racing across the field to first base before one of us tagged her. We didn't have much, but Ma made it feel like we had it all.

By the time I came out of the bathroom, John had already fixed Ma's lunch and gave her a dose of the *Pepto-Bismol*.

I started cleaning up the makeshift kitchen, avoiding Ma's eyes on me.

"Why you be holed up in that bathroom so much?"

With my back still to her, I said, "I just haven't been feeling so well, is all."

I could feel Ma giving me that look she always gave me since I was old enough to understand what that look meant: *I'm your mama and you my child. I know when somethin' ailin' you.*

It was no less than what I expected: Ma to be the one sick but more worried about trying to take care of me.

I busied myself straightening up the room, putting away stuff that didn't need putting away. I just couldn't face Ma, couldn't let her see me this way. I needed to be strong. For her. For us. For me.

"We better get going or we're going to be late."

Ma tried to hold my eyes, but I quickly turned away and rushed to get her things and Nancy, before we marched slowly once again to our *asylum*.

THE HOLY GHOST

I never understood how these two words could work together:
holy *and* ghost. *Whether you believe or not, there will come*
a time when your faith and your fears will collide, and the
only thing you will have to turn to is your own holy ghost.

I am sitting on a black Lutyens garden bench. There are lush plants and trees spreading out in every direction and the most beautiful animals I have ever seen. They are all around me. I can hear water. Then I can see it, cascading down a bank of rocks. I stare at it—the water, the animals, the birds, the trees—and I feel at peace. The peace moves around me and through me. I don't feel alone. I don't feel afraid. I don't feel the pain. It has gone away. It has left me. I don't understand why. I don't understand how. But the pain is gone and the birds and the water and the trees are my sanctuary. And the pain has left me. It has gone away, and I don't understand how.

I don't understand why.

I bolted upright, clutching my chest. The room was dark, my breath heavy. I was sweating and my T-shirt was damp. My eyes adjusted to the darkness, and I looked over at the bed next to mine. Ma and John were lying there, their backs to me. I didn't see Nancy, but I could hear her. I could hear her and Ma breathing.

I lay back down and turned toward the window, the light that shined through. I didn't want to close my eyes. I didn't want to sleep. I didn't want to feel that kind of peace.

The tears slid onto my pillow. My breath slowed, my heart stopped racing, and I could smell the sulfuric acidy bleach that permeated from the sheets. I didn't want to close my eyes. I didn't want to sleep.

I eased out of the bed and silently fumbled around the dark room to find my jeans, a sweatshirt, and my sneakers. Then I looked for my backpack with my laptop. The moment I opened the door, the hall lights shocked my eyes. The hotel was quiet at just past 3:00 a.m., except for the muffled sounds of footsteps and a door opening and closing in the distance. I headed to the lobby, and when I got there, there was a young woman sitting behind the desk. I nodded at her and she smiled at me because she knew where I was headed, over to one of the high-top tables in the corner, to the place I had been going every day to find solace. I unloaded my backpack and opened my laptop and waited for it to fire up. Already my mind began to ease, and I felt a calm come over me as I opened the file to my next book, *A Life Apart*, a historical novel about an interracial love triangle that spanned decades—a story I had come to take refuge in.

As soon as my fingers touched the keyboard, it was like a switch had turned on and suddenly everything that was real and honest and true disappeared, and I was in a world where there was no pain, that I could control, that I could change.

And I escaped.

Until darkness faded and the sun began to spread out all around me. An array of orange and yellow permeated throughout the lobby, giving life to the cozy room. I'd been writing for nearly three hours before dawn pulled me back out of that world and into my own. I looked around, and there were people already lined up at the desk and having breakfast in the dining space across the lobby. I've always loved watching people—the way they stand or walk or talk. I often found myself staring at someone, wondering if they were facing anything capable of breaking their heart. Some of them were smiling. Some were talking. Some had no expression at all. I wondered about those people—the *expressionless*: what was on their minds, what they could be going through. At moments, I imagined that I must look like one of them.

After a while, I packed up my stuff and made my way back to the room. The room was still dark and quiet, and Ma and John were still sleeping. I went into the bathroom and took a long shower. I thought about the dream again. It was *so* real. I was there, in that place where everything seemed peaceful. I closed my eyes and let the warm water cascade down my back the way the water cascaded down those rocks in my dream.

I finally stepped out of the shower, dried off, and splashed cold water on my face. I brushed my teeth, then put back on the same jeans, sweatshirt, and sneakers and opened the door to find Ma sitting on the edge of the bed with Nancy next to her.

"Good morning. Let me help you into the bathroom."

Ma raised up her hand at me. "I'm fine. I can make it."

I watched her sit for a while then slowly make her way into the bathroom. I stood there until I heard the water and her heavy breaths again. Then I went over to the makeshift kitchen and started breakfast—eggs, whole grain bagel, Swiss cheese, and grapefruit. I sprinkled some turmeric on her eggs because I'd read somewhere that turmeric can kill cancer cells and prevent more from growing. I doused the eggs, once, twice, and then again.

When Ma finally came out of the bathroom, she took a seat at the small table and looked down at the food.

"I'm not hungry this morning."

"I know, Ma, but you must eat to keep up your strength."

"Why you keep putting that stuff on my food?"

I looked at the eggs. It was a bit much. "It's good for you, Ma. It helps kill the cancer."

Ma got a serious look on her face. "Ain't nothin' gonna kill no cancer but God."

I thought about the first time I saw Ma get the Holy Ghost. Ma had taken us kids to a church near Point Breeze Avenue, about twelve blocks from our house in Wilson Park Projects in Philadelphia. Though it was a modest-looking Baptist church, it seemed that everyone south and north of Point Breeze Avenue was there. All kinds of people—whole families, single moms with their children, men who looked like they'd just stepped out of a bar still reeking of alcohol, children who came just to pass the time, teenage boys with do-rags on their heads. Ma said it didn't matter how people showed up at church, as long as they *showed up*. It may not have mattered with other kids, but Ma made sure our clothes and hair were always pressed. She even shined our faces with Vaseline.

When we got there, we were greeted at the wide plank doors by elderly ladies in all white—white dresses, fancy white hats, white gloves, white stockings. Even the program they handed to us at the door was white! All five of us smiled at the nice ladies and followed Ma down the center of the aisle to a pew that could fit us all. We filed into our seats and just stared ahead; we knew better than to embarrass Ma. She always gave us a tongue-lashing before she took us anywhere.

I took notice of all the people who were flocking into the church like they were marching toward an asylum. Ma had told us once that people came to church every Sunday for two things: to praise God and to get *hope*. I knew Ma was right because that was the only time I had ever seen so many people coming together no matter where or how they lived. It was like we were all one gigantic family. Strangers hugging and shaking hands. And when the pastor took to the podium and started a slow fiery drawl about *holding on*, something magical happened. People started jumping to their feet, their hands raised toward the high ceilings, and some started to cry. And then one woman in the pew right in front of us started shouting, thrashing about and speaking in some strange language. Two of the ladies in white had to hold her arms to keep her from hurting herself. I got a little scared for her—and for me. Then I looked over at Ma and watched her transform, too, right before my eyes. She started crying and shaking and thrashing about like she was in a trance. I was so confused 'cause I'd hardly ever seen Ma cry before—except once when our daddy didn't come home on payday and Ma had to feed us hungry kids Argo cornstarch, and later at Daddy's funeral.

Now, when we arrived at the clinic and the young doctor came into the room, I completely expected him to say, *Your mother's been cured.* Instead, he looked at us and said, "So now we wait to see what happens. You can go home."

"Go home? And wait? Wait for what?"

The young doctor thumbed through Ma's file, looking for what he was already prepared to tell us. That the latest tests confirmed that Ma's DNA was the same and that it would take some time before we would see if she was responding to the *Pepto-Bismol.*

"The nurse will be in to walk you through how to dispense the treatments to your mother, and I'll be following up with a weekly call to check on her. At least you'll get to make it home in time for Christmas."

I had all but forgotten that Christmas Eve was only two days away. I looked over at Ma, tried to smile, but she didn't smile back.

"Do you have any more questions for me?"

John spoke up. "So, what you're saying is that if we go home and as long as she keeps taking that medicine that there's a chance we can still beat this, right?"

I looked closely at the young doctor.

He leaned back in his chair, and he looked at John and then over at me. "Each patient is different. We can't always be sure, but what I can tell you is that many of our patients have responded well to the treatment. Your mother's cancer is progressive, and it's hard to say right now how well she will respond. Let's just keep up with the treatments and monitor her."

I looked past him and out the window, at nothing.

The doctor stood from his seat. "I'll send the nurse in, and she will prepare everything you need to take home with you."

I stared at him. His eyes were compassionate and sad and disappointed and hopeful and honest. They were so many things, I didn't know what to believe.

He left the room, and I glanced at Ma again. "Well, at least you'll get to spend Christmas in your new home."

Ma looked past me and out the window, her face expression-less, mixed with something I had never seen before.

"I'm ready to go home. I want to go home."

We sat there for a while with nothing more to be said between us before we slowly walked out of the Burzynski Clinic to take Ma home.

NO CHARGE

I once heard someone say that when you are at your lowest point, life will defy all that you knew to be true and the only things you will have to fall back on are those lessons you learned as a child.

M a lay in the bed in a flannel nightgown and thick white socks. The room was dark, shadowed against the heavy draperies. A litany of brown bottles—different shapes and sizes with white caps and labels—was on the nightstand with a glass of water. It wasn't long after we returned from Houston that she refused to take the *Pepto-Bismol*. I was beginning to get frustrated with her. I wanted her to take off that flannel nightgown and those ugly white socks and get out of that bed! I wanted her to fight! The way she had fought all of her life.

I gazed at Ma lying there with her eyes closed as Shirley Caesar's sultry gospel voice oozed from a CD player sitting in the corner near Nancy. Aunt Deller sat opposite me in the chair next to Ma's bed. We took turns taking care of Ma. Me, Aunt Deller, and John. Almost a spitting image of her, Aunt Deller was Ma's closest sister—so close that Ma and John chose to buy their retirement home in Lugoff, a small town not far from Columbia, South Carolina, where Aunt Deller and Uncle Bobby lived. They'd saved up all their life to pay for the quaint home that we brought Ma to live in for the first time when we left Houston. I couldn't help but think about all the floors and toilets Ma had to scrub, the countless things she had to go without to afford the charming home that was twice as big and fancy as any home she'd ever lived in or owned.

Ma had only stepped foot in that house three times: the day she fell in love with it when we went house hunting, the day they settled on the house, and the day we brought her home from

Houston. By then, Ma could only take a few steps before she lost her breath and had to be escorted in. My heart *broke*. Ma deserved that house, and it wasn't fair! It just *was not fair* that this was the way that she was to live in it.

Now, Ma lay in the bed with her eyes closed, humming to Shirley Caesar and refusing to eat or take the *Pepto-Bismol*. I was trying desperately not to say what I was thinking. I knew Ma couldn't help it because she was so sick. But I also knew that the only way she would live was if *she* wanted to live.

There was no science or theory or happenstance that could explain what was happening. It wasn't even something I could make out in my consciousness. There would be no consciousness without Ma. Every breath I'd taken since she brought me into the world was nourished by knowing that Ma would always be there.

I wanted to yell. I wanted to scream. I wanted to howl: *Get Up! Get Up! Get Up!*

I sat there in silence wrestling with my anguished thoughts until I couldn't stand it anymore. I left the room and went into the kitchen to call Houston. Someone needed to tell me something.

I dialed the number I had memorized, and the moment I heard the receptionist's voice on the other end, I barked at her.

"I'd like to speak to my mother's doctor, now!"

She put me on hold for a long while before patching me through to the doctor.

"You've been calling every week, but you always say the same thing. I want to know what's going on. Is this treatment helping my mother or not?"

I did not cry. I was too angry to cry.

"I'm glad you called. I was planning to give you a call today to let you know that we reviewed your mother's latest pathology report, and we have noticed a slight adjustment in her cells."

"Really? What does that mean?"

I heard papers shuffling.

"It means that your mother may be finally responding to the treatment."

I felt the tension in my body ease. "So it means that she's getting better?"

"Well, we're not quite there yet. We still have a ways to go. But at least her test results are looking better."

After I hung up the phone, I rushed into Ma's bedroom.

"I just spoke to the doctor. He said you're doing much better. The treatment is working!"

Ma looked at me with the same look she had since we returned from Houston. "That treatment ain't doin' me no good. It's making me more sick."

I stood there staring at Ma, my emotions raw. In the past hour alone, I had gone from anger to anguish to grief to hope. I was an emotional wreck!

"Why you got to be so negative? All you do is lay in that bed feeling sorry for yourself! Why won't you get up and get dressed so you can get better?"

"Who you raisin' your voice at?!"

I held Ma's eyes, refusing to look away. I had never raised my voice to my mother, and I didn't mean to do it now. But I needed her to fight! We stared at each other for a long time until I stormed out of the room and grabbed the keys to Ma's car. I wasn't sure where I was going or what I was going to do. I just drove around in circles until I ended up in the Walmart parking lot. There weren't too many other places to go in Lugoff.

I parked the car at the far end of the lot, and I sat there for a while thinking once again about how Ma could be so healthy one day and end up with Stage IV terminal cancer the next. Then out of the blue—out of the crazy dang blue—I rested my head on the steering wheel, tears, snot, and all pouring from every pore of my face and just started singing "No Charge."

Whenever us kids acted up or got on what Ma called her *last nerve,* she would make us all sit on the living room sofa, from youngest to oldest, put Shirley Caesar's vinyl album on the record console, and play "No Charge"—a song about a little boy who gave his mother a list of what she owed him for doing his chores.

"Ya'll ain't movin' from that couch till you learn. Ya'll gonna appreciate the way I raised you when you have to raise your own chi'ren," Ma would say. Sometimes we'd have to sit there for hours, not a word between us, listening to that song play over and over and over again.

"Tough love," Ma called it.

It was her *tough love* that I'd carried with me for years to come, the thing that I'd reached back on to get me through some of the most difficult times of my life.

Now, it was me and "No Charge" in the Walmart parking lot in Ma's little blue Kia. I kept singing that song until my head felt like it was going to explode. And I didn't care. I wanted to explode. I wanted to see Ma again in that beautiful lace dress she wore to my wedding. I wanted to stand shoulder to shoulder with her once more at the kitchen sink, cleaning collard greens. I wanted to taste the fried fish that she made for me every time I came for a visit. I wanted to see her get the Holy Ghost. I wanted to sit on that couch for hours listening to "No Charge."

I was emotionally exhausted by the time I realized I'd been in the Walmart parking lot for more than an hour. I needed to get back to Ma. It was well past time for her lunch. I found some napkins in the glove compartment and did the best I could to clean my face before I headed back to the house.

When I went inside, I was surprised to find John, Aunt Deller, and Ma sitting in the living room. Ma was dressed in a pair of khaki capris, a white cotton blouse, and a new pair of white socks.

"I want you to fry me some fish for dinner. I ain't had no fish in a long time."

I teared up again. For the first time in months, Ma looked like *hope*.

"Yes, Ma. I'm gonna go to the fish market and buy some fresh fish, and then I'm gonna fry you some of the best fish you've ever had. I'm gonna fry you some fish, Ma."

As I turned to leave, I knew that though she didn't have the strength to get out of that bed, she did it for the reasons she had done everything in her life.

She did it for me. She did it for us. She did it for her family.

HER FAMILY

Family. There's nothing more to be said . . .

I stood next to Anthony, same height and age, our small hands grasping the clothed edges of the casket. We were five years old. "Would you like to see your daddy?" The man's voice was kind as he lifted us up at the same time and tilted us into the casket. I cried. I knew something was terribly wrong with the way Ma stood closely behind, two-year-old Angie clinging to her black dress, Roy Jr. and Eileen by her side.

I don't remember him much . . . just the way he played with us, always in his dark blue khaki uniform, the smell of sweat and hard work pulsing from his pores. His laugh, so robust and raw. I knew he adored his family. Then *why*, I often heard my small mind wondering, *Why* was Ma always crying? *Why* the ugly scars on her face, the knife wound on her leg? *Why*, his voice like music to my small ears was sometimes suddenly so bitter?

It was March 1973, the day so many conflicting emotions floated through my delicate heart. But I knew one thing for sure: Daddy wasn't coming home anymore, and Ma—though now faced with raising five children on her own—would never have to cry that way again.

I was six when John showed up. He was quiet but kind. I could tell by the way he always spoke to Ma, his voice tempered, the way he looked at her. For the nearly forty years that they'd been together, I can't recall a time I ever saw John raise his voice to Ma, let alone hurt her. In fact, I don't know too many men who would accept an abused woman with five small children and raise them as his own. John cherished Ma, and I imagined that he felt a little sad for her, all the abuse that she'd suffered from my grandfather and my father. The way my grandfather had forced her and her siblings to strip to the nude, then inflict lashes from a thick leather belt until he drew blood. The way he had beaten my grandmother.

Ma said by the time my daddy showed up and picked up where Granddaddy had left off, her nerves were so bad that she shook like a leaf. Those were her words: *shook like a leaf.* I often wondered what it looked like: Ma shaking like a leaf, blowing in the wind. *Just blowing.*

Years later, I *would* soon come to know.

"Ya'll ain't having no boy company in my house till you turn sixteen." That's what Ma told us girls since we were old enough to notice boys. I couldn't wait to turn sixteen, especially after Eileen was the first to have her boy company since she was three years older than me. I'd sit in the living room across from Eileen and her boy company, just watching and waiting.

By the time I turned sixteen, I already had him picked out. He was seventeen, charming, and one of the cutest boys I'd ever met. He knew just how to say all the right things to make me feel special. So months later when he went into a jealous rage because he thought I was seeing another boy, I didn't see the punch coming. He promised that it would never happen again, that he'd done it because he loved me so much. The next time came not too long after. This time, I told myself that I was leaving. But his remorse sent a fierce strike of lightning right to my heart, making it swell with forgiveness. Then the next time, he cried so hard that I cried too. And the next time. And the next time. And the next time. Until I found myself knocked up and shaking like a leaf too. By the time I graduated high school and had my baby, I finally managed to move as far away as I could get from him and Wilson Park and enroll in community college where I took classes at night while Ma watched the baby.

By then, I'd made a decision that I never again wanted that kind of *boy company*. An education was going to be my way out! The more classes I took, the more knowledge I consumed, the more it would shield me, I thought, from ever letting another man beat me like that again. I worked a full-time job, went to school at night, and occasionally took part-time jobs on the weekends to raise my daughter as a single mother. I worked, went to school, and raised my daughter. I worked, went to school, and raised my daughter. I worked, went to school, and raised my daughter all the while nursing a string of failed relationships and marriages with behavior that bordered on verbal and emotional abuse. I earned three degrees, each one paving the way to a career that gave me a rite of passage to the American dream—in my case, driving my daughter to college.

It hadn't occurred to me that, years later, Treasure, my own daughter, would come to know what it felt like to shake like a leaf too. The first time she showed me the scars on her neck, my heart stopped. "Mom, he's going to kill me," she said to me as calmly and stoically as if she had just said, "I'm going to the mall to get some ice cream." As though I hadn't done all I knew how to do to protect her from ever having to utter those words. Didn't I work my ass off to keep her from that kind of *boy company?* Hadn't she known about her daddy, my daddy, and Ma's daddy? Didn't she read *Color Me Butterfly?*

I closed my eyes and tried to shut out the scars that I saw on her neck, the fear I heard in her voice.

"You deserve better! You deserve better!" I just kept repeating those words as though I was reaching back into generation after generation.

The scars on her neck would be the start of a tumultuous and reckless relationship that forced her to move to Philadelphia to live with Ma. Then he'd find her and they'd shack up until she started shaking like a leaf again and we'd call the police, get a restraining order, and try to talk some sense into her. The *sense* lasted only long enough until they'd shack up again and she'd shake like a leaf and we'd call the police, get a restraining order, and try to talk some sense into her—again and again and again until Ma and I found ourselves at Pennsylvania Hospital watching her, with him standing inches away from me, push out a 6-pound, 11-ounce baby girl they named Promise.

Six months later, I'd reached back on Ma's *tough love* to draw strength as I sat across from Treasure once again, her face swollen and scars around her neck, as she told me how he'd strangled her until she began to black out, and it was because she heard Promise screaming that she fought—to save Promise.

I cried. I didn't know what else to do. I'd said all I knew how to say, had done all I knew how to do. This fight was bigger than me, stronger than me, more powerful than me. Even Ma's tough love was no match for this.

The next morning, I hadn't planned to write the letter I wrote until I started writing it. I needed someone to help me, to help *us*.

August 25, 2007
Dear Oprah,
This morning, I am writing to you in a time of duress.
I come from a family of women who has endured 60+ years of domestic violence and abuse. The abuse stemmed from my grandmother, to my mother, to myself, and now my daughter, who is currently 22 years old and is in a horrendously abusive relationship, one that has threatened her life many times . . .
I'm writing you today because I learned that my daughter's boyfriend tried to kill her again last night and although I've done everything in my power to try to help her, she just won't listen. And deep in my heart I know as a mother and domestic violence advocate, that it's not that she won't listen, but that she's living in fear. And what breaks my heart even more is that she now has a six-month-old daughter named Promise.

Not only has this man tried to kill my daughter several times, but he has also threatened to kill Promise . . . . I can't even explain the depth of pain in my heart when I heard this. I feel helpless because the current laws offer no recourse for the victim's family and I should not have to wait until this man follows through on his actions before the laws will protect them.

Why am I writing to you about this? Well, I've decided that although my daughter won't listen, I must do something to save Promise and hopefully by saving Promise I will save my only daughter as well. I plan to launch the "Saving Promise" campaign . . .

I pray that you will help me with the Saving Promise campaign. My hope is that by bringing national attention to this, that perhaps someone will LISTEN and maybe I can change the laws and save my daughter's and Promise's life.

In closing, I live daily with the fear of "that" phone call. The one that will tell me he finally prevailed. I hope and pray that I'm able to do something to change this for Promise and my daughter and for the countless other women and children living a life of fear.

L.Y. Marlow

I mailed a copy of that letter along with a photo of Promise to every one of Oprah's producers. I didn't really expect to hear back. But I recalled a story about a woman who had shared on Oprah's show about how she had bought a pair of Oprah's shoes at a charity sale and whenever she got really depressed and didn't have anyone to talk to, she would take out Oprah's shoes and stand in them.

I felt like that woman, like I had no one to talk to, nowhere to turn. I *needed* to stand in Oprah's shoes, *any* shoes other than my own. Later, I would come to understand that even if Oprah had tried to help, she would have unknowingly preempted the lessons I was to learn.

Within a few days, I'd launched Saving Promise—a national domestic violence nonprofit organization that would provide greater public education, prevention programs, and policies. I didn't care that I didn't know the first thing about running a nonprofit or any business for that matter. I was operating on sheer fate and fear, taking everything I owned, every cent I had and investing it into Saving Promise. I hired attorneys and accountants to help me set up the organization and people to help me run it.

Though I knew very little about what I was doing, I had a few things going for myself: 1) the hard knocks of life growing up in Wilson Park Projects, 2) I'd not only survived a very abusive relationship but had a family history of it, so technically that qualified me as an expert in the subject matter, and 3) I had sixteen years of education, which landed me an MBA *and* I was clawing my way up the corporate ladder, convinced that I was going to shatter somebody's glass ceiling, if not my own. Hell, how hard could it be?

Since I was in the second grade, I always had a gift for wrangling people together and getting them to be on *my* team. I'd stand in the schoolyard and gather two, sometimes three of my classmates and sketch out a plan for how we were going to solve the math problem that Mrs. Lanaham had given us just before recess. I hated math and I was terrible at it, but I had a knack for solving problems. The numbers were just a part of a problem that needed to be solved. No big deal. So I'd get a few other mediocre kids together and convince them that three brains were better than one. That was it. That was my strategy. No secrets. No Einstein voodoo. And nine out of ten times, it worked!

So the way that I approached my second-grade lessons would ultimately become the way I approached Saving Promise and solving one of the biggest global health crises of our time.

It was *very* hard. Dorothy was no longer in Kansas or in Mrs. Lanaham's class.

Shit!

First, I was fast running out of money and no one wanted to give me funding. Who cared that I had developed a passion out of sheer fate and fear, had some ballsy strategic ideas about how to solve this *thing*, and that my family had survived more than sixty years of domestic violence? I'd soon come to discover that the *kids* in the playground were not the same kids in Mrs.

Lanaham's class. They were much bigger, and they had drawn invisible dividing lines in the sandbox that I wasn't allowed to cross.

This line and the one that I was sketching on my own went on for years, until I found myself on the brink of financial, physical, emotional, and spiritual bankruptcy—not to mention I was going through yet another divorce, and that little bastard called *cancer* had decided to attack Ma and wreak havoc on my already tenuous existence, and as if that wasn't bad enough, my whole team suddenly decided to quit on me—and Saving Promise!

Quitting wasn't enough to stick the knife in my already fragile heart. They all decided to submit their resignations at the same time—the deputy director, the public relations manager, and my executive assistant. Here I was, hundreds of miles away, trying to save Ma, and I received one email after another with little more than *I resign.*

Everything that I ever contrived about humanity and compassion had escaped me. This *beast* was nothing like the trick monster I saw transform from a woman into an ape at that vintage show when I was eight years old. This beast was *real.* But as real as it was, Ma needed me.

So the divorce, the looming bankruptcy, the cruel people, Saving Promise, and even Oprah (if she should finally happen to call) would just have to wait.

WALKING TO HEAVEN
FOR HOPE

There's an old adage that says people need three things to be happy: Someone to love, something to do . . . and something to hope for.

I lay on the cot next to Ma's hospital bed listening to her all night, my heart breaking into tiny pieces.

"Take me, God. Take me, Lord. Please take me . . . Take me, Lord. Take me, God. Please take me . . . Take me now, Lord. Please, God, take me. Please, God, take me . . . please take me."

She had been doing so well those first few weeks after fish night—sitting in the living room in front of the fireplace, talking, and eating. The young doctor had called again to say Ma was getting better, and even Nancy no longer had to follow us everywhere we went. Then one night Ma woke up with a 103-degree fever, and we had to rush her to the hospital. The doctor said that the cancer was spreading rapidly, and Ma had to go back on the chemo.

I didn't know what to do.

On one hand, I wanted Ma to get better, even if it meant they had to treat her with the chemo. On the other hand, I didn't want them putting that poison back in her. Then the doctor showed us Ma's X-rays, how the cancer was spreading. I hated those fuckers! Growing inside Ma, hurting her. I wanted them gone! I wanted them out of her!

We agreed to the treatment, and within a week, we took Ma home. But a few weeks later when Ma woke up in the middle of the night screaming, I regretted that decision.

Now, I lay there on the small cot, listening to Ma chanting until I could take no more.

"Ma, please, please don't say that! We can beat this! Please, Ma, ask God to save you, not take you. Please, Ma, please."

Ma didn't even try to open her eyes. "Please, God, take me, God. Please. Take me, Lord, please take me."

I left the room and rushed down the hall to the nurses' station.

"You need to do something! Isn't there something you can give her for the pain?"

The two nurses looked up at me, and one of them said, "Ma'am, we've given her everything we can give her. There's nothing more we can do for her."

Shaking, I looked at that nurse like she had two heads. "How dare you! How dare you say that to me! There's always something you can do! That's not your mother in that room screaming for God to take her! She's mine! And while she's in this hospital, you're gonna take good care of her! Do you hear me, bitch?! In fact, I want my mother out of this hospital! I want to transfer her now!"

The other nurse stood up. "Ma'am, we're sorry. That's not what she meant. Of course, we want to take good care of your mother. I'm gonna call the doctor right now and see what we can do. Okay?"

My glare shifted from the first nurse, and I looked at her for a long time, just standing there, shaken.

"Yes. I'd like for you to call the doctor. Please call him."

She held my eyes, and I could tell in that moment, she wasn't just a nurse. She was her mother's daughter, and she recognized that little girl who stood in front of her, begging for them to save *her* mother.

"Why don't you go downstairs to the lounge and get some tea. I'm gonna call the doctor right now. Okay?"

I looked down the hall toward Ma's room before I turned in the opposite direction and walked toward the elevator.

I found a quiet and quaint sitting area where no one was around and just sat there, too tense to have tea. I needed some quiet time to myself to get my head together. I wasn't ready to go back to Ma's room and hear her beg for mercy. A mercy that made me realize that she was in so much pain that she'd rather die. The thought of it scared me beyond measure. I never considered that Ma would die. It was insurmountable to me, the thought of her dying. Losing Ma would mean that there would be no more family gatherings, no Sunday dinners, no rational and encouraging voice on the other end of the line when I called, as I often did. More than that, my life would not be a life without Ma as far as I was concerned.

Later, when I returned to the floor, the nurse told me that the doctor had prescribed pain medication to help Ma sleep. I went back into the room and watched her as she slept, a peace on her face that looked part relieved and part distressed. I couldn't tell how she was feeling or what she may have been thinking or dreaming, only that she was finally sleeping.

The next morning when the doctor came and examined her, he informed us that she had pneumonia. An infection in both lungs that has caused fluid to build, making it difficult for her to breathe, and then arranged to have the fluid drained from her lungs.

A little while later, an escort showed up to take Ma to the radiologist who would perform the procedure. I told the *nice* nurse that I wanted to be with Ma when they performed the procedure.

Walking down the corridor, onto the elevator, and through a set of flapping doors that led to the radiology department was like walking to heaven for hope. Hope that the radiologist who was removing the fluid from Ma's lungs was going to drain her of whatever made her scream those words through the night.

When they pushed Ma's bed through a door that led to the room where they were going to perform the procedure, I was on the heels of Ma's bed before the escort stopped me.

"You have to wait out here."

I stared him down. "I'm going in that room with my mother."

"Ma'am, you can't go inside. Please take a seat, and when they're done, they will let you see your mother."

"I need to talk to the radiologist. Please get him for me."

I could tell that the escort was annoyed with me, but I didn't care. When the radiologist came out, I didn't need to explain all that had happened, nor why I had called him out there. He just said, "It's fine if you want to come inside and be with your mother. But I must warn you that it could be very difficult to watch."

"I understand."

He nodded and motioned for me to follow him. When I entered the room, Ma was lying on a table with a sheet covering her up to her chest. I smiled at her, and she just looked at me, tired.

I took a seat in the chair in the corner next to the tall IV pole that had four different intravenous bags dripping white, yellow, and grayish fluids into Ma. For a minute I thought, *It's no wonder Ma needs fluid drained from her.*

Moments later, the radiologist accompanied by a nurse started the procedure. After giving Ma something to numb her chest, he took a wide needle that was attached to a long tube and inserted it through the side of Ma's chest. Instantly, streams of mucus mixed with dark blood started to drain through the tube into a large liter-sized plastic bag. It took no time to fill up two bags.

Looking at those bags was like looking at Ma's life passing right before me. I felt the tears sliding down my face, felt my own chest tighten.

Minutes later, the radiologist removed the needle from Ma's chest, then walked over to the small sink and started washing his hands.

I wiped my tears and stood up. "Did you drain it all? I mean, is all the fluid gone?"

The doctor stopped washing his hands and grabbed a paper towel to dry them. "We drained as much as we can today, but we can't drain too much at one time because it can cause her lungs to collapse. But we got enough of it to release the pressure so she can breathe easier."

I looked over at Ma. Already I could tell she was breathing better.

"Thank you." I said it with enough intensity that he knew it meant so much more to me than those two words could express.

The doctor patted me on the back and told us that the escort would return soon to take Ma back to her room.

Over the next few days, Ma got better. She was even sitting up and watching TV and talking to me, John, and Aunt Deller. I called Eileen, Roy Jr., and Anthony and told them that Ma was feeling better and it would be good for her to see them. They all agreed to come the following weekend, and Eileen agreed to stay with Ma in the hospital while I flew back to my home in Maryland. I had not noticed how much weight I'd lost, just how very sick I'd become myself from the emotional stress of it all. I was exhausted, and I needed time to reinvigorate my spirit.

The morning that I was leaving to fly home, I sat in a chair next to Ma's bed and watched the gospel channel, listening to her hum the words to some of her favorite songs.

"I guess you got a lot of work to do when you get back home, huh?"

I turned and looked at Ma. "Yes. But it's fine. I'll get caught up."

Ma got quiet for a while. Then she turned to me again, removed the mask from her face, and said, "You know I'm proud of you, right?"

I looked at Ma, surprised. She wasn't one to express herself like that. She hardly ever said those kinds of words, always one to show us how she felt rather than tell us.

"Yes, I know, Ma."

"I just want you to know that no matter what happens to me, I want you to keep doin' what you're doin'. You hear me?"

"Ma, we don't need to talk about that right now. I'm just glad you're feeling better."

"You hear what I'm sayin'? I'm proud of you, and you keep doin' what you're doin'. Everything, you hear?"

There was something different about the way Ma looked at me, the way her eyes held mine. I held her gaze, then said, "Okay, Ma. I will. I promise."

We looked at each other for a while, then Ma said, "You better go and call that slowpoke before he make you miss your flight. You know how slow he is."

I smiled at Ma before stepping out into the hall to call John. When I returned, I settled back into my seat, closed my eyes, and listened to the gospel music against the sweet sounds of Ma's soft hum that floated through her oxygen mask.

MY REFUGE

It is important to have a sacred place—a safe haven—where you can rest your mind, body, heart, and soul and embrace all that life has to offer.

The moment I got home, I shut the door behind me and took in the solitude of my sanctuary—a quaint apartment in the historical district of Ellicott City, Maryland. I was finally alone, all alone. I dropped my bags by the door, kicked off my shoes, and headed into my bedroom to undress, take a long hot shower, and wash my hair. Then I threw on a pair of sweats, my boots, jacket, and a hat and walked around the back of the complex to the rolling, rocky river forested by trees that ran alongside a train track, where a freight train passed through every few hours. There was a crisp chill in the air and remnants of snow from a recent snowfall, much different from the mild weather in Lugoff. I took a seat on a bench just steps away from the river, bundled my jacket around me, closed my eyes, and got lost in the sounds of the rushing water and the fresh scent of the crisp air.

The river had been my refuge since I walked away from a loveless marriage to discover the woman who had been defined by a string of endless broken relationships and a career at IBM that I was beginning to loathe. Beyond the name that Ma gave me, I really didn't know who I was. The first night I moved into my apartment, I sat on the living room floor with my CD player and a bottle of wine. My furniture was scheduled to arrive the next day, and I didn't care because I just wanted to take in what was now *my* room, bare of the expensive furnishings and collectibles that had filled the brand-new home I'd shared with my husband for more than five years. We had built a life around the make-believe exterior that we were the perfect couple—both immersed in careers with salaries that afforded us an expensive home, luxury cars, and enough money in the bank to more than sustain the quiet but lavish lifestyle we'd built together.

Our first few years were good, mainly because I always thought this was what I was *supposed* to have—a beautiful home, a progressive career, and a man who made me feel safe. But I had just turned forty, and it was like my biological clock shifted. Not the clock that craved babies and bibs, but the clock that ticked away at my soul. I'd been sleepwalking most of my adult life and suddenly there was the universe shouting through a bullhorn: *Wake Up. Wake the Hell Up!* And I'd woken up too, nearly every day laboring over the decision whether to stay or leave. Just throw on some jeans and walk out the front door. Walk away from the life I'd worked so hard to build. I was just plain tired of living the fairytale story that we are taught as little girls about the big castle and Prince Charming.

After I had invested so much time and money in perfecting my castle, no sooner had the new smells faded, than my love for it faded too. I hated that house, and my Prince Charming had changed too. I began to think that maybe, just maybe, he hadn't changed at all. Maybe I just created a false image of him as part of the shaky foundation on which we had built our lives. But we both knew something was wrong. I'd been crying and begging and pleading for things to change, for *us* to change. He was beginning to squeeze the joy right out of me. But how could I walk away now? Hadn't I prayed for this life? *For him?* And didn't I believe in the sanctity of marriage? I'd watched Ma and John stick it out for nearly forty years. And Ma always said you're supposed to stay through *thick and thin*. But this was more *thick* than I had signed up for. Besides which, one year prior, I had published *Color Me Butterfly*. Reliving the stories of my grandmother, my mother, myself, and my daughter was like going through a metamorphosis—transforming the woman who was busting at the seams of a fictional existence. I was no longer the same person I'd been when I'd stood shoulder to shoulder with my husband-to-be under a beautiful turquoise sky in St. Lucia in a breezy white dress, a white flower in my hair, barefoot in the warm sand, bluish-green ocean crashing behind us, and said words that would come to haunt me.

I just didn't want to be married anymore.

So one evening, I walked downstairs into the man cave where my husband spent most of his time and confessed: *I can't do this no more.* Then I graciously walked back upstairs to the master bedroom with all the luxuries I'd spent the last year creating and moved my toothbrush and clothes into the guest bedroom. Nearly one year later, I finally found the courage to move into a one-bedroom apartment.

Now, I just sat staring at the river, thinking about all that I'd been through the last few years. I was so emotionally, physically, and spiritually exhausted that I didn't know what made me more sad: my life or Ma. In many ways, my life was no different from Ma's cancer—seemingly healthy cells that suddenly change into toxic little creatures that sneak up on you one day and snatch your life away. Just snatch it without any regard for who you are or who you think you are. My little creatures were everything that had brought me to now: another failed marriage, a career I no longer loved, an aspiring career as an author that left me starving for more than that next great American novel, and an organization that took more than I could give and was faltering by the minute.

Dread and sorrow tore at my heart.

I hovered in the brisk cold watching the river brush against the rocks until my toes and fingers became numb, and then headed back upstairs to call the hospital to check on Ma and see if Eileen, Roy Jr., and Anthony had arrived.

Anthony and his wife were there, and Eileen and Roy Jr. were still on the way.

I told Anthony everything he needed to know about the hospital, the nurses, Ma's doctors, and how much better Ma was doing after they drained the fluid from her lungs.

After I hung up the phone, I changed into my pajamas, closed all the window blinds, crawled into my bed, and pulled the comforter over my head and slept.

Slept like I hadn't slept in months.

For the next few days in between trying to get caught up on my work with Saving Promise, borrowing time to write, and nursing the flu that had invaded my body within hours of returning home, I called the hospital at least three times a day to check on Ma. I was glad that Eileen was there with her now, but I could tell that it was already taking a toll on her.

"Did Ma say those things all night when you were here?"

I pressed the phone to my ear, alarmed. "What things?"

Eileen lowered her voice. I imagined her on the cot in the corner across from Ma's bed where I'd slept.

"Mumbling *Please take me, Lord. Take me.*"

I stood up from my seat quickly. "When did she start that again?"

"Last night. I was asleep, and it woke me up."

"Has she been complaining of any pain?"

"Not really. She just kept talking about being tired and wanting it to be over. Then last night she started saying those words all night long."

I could feel the pressure of the phone pressed against my ear. I closed my eyes.

"If Ma died, I don't know if I could go on without her."

"Don't say that, Eileen! Ma's going to be alright. She was feeling better when they drained the fluid from her lungs, and before she was admitted to the hospital, the doctors in Houston said her condition was improving. Now we got to be strong. She's going to get through this. We just got to be strong."

I heard Eileen sigh. There was a long silence, then I could hear people talking in the background.

"Who's that?"

"The doctor's here. He came to examine Ma because I told the nurse about what happened last night and she called the doctor. I have to go."

"Please ask the doctor to call me after he's finished examining her."

After we hung up, I rushed into my bedroom and pulled the familiar carry-on luggage from my closet and started throwing anything I could find into it while I looked for my purse to grab my credit card to book a flight. For the last several months I had been moving so much between Maryland, Philadelphia, Houston, Lugoff, and hospital after hospital that I didn't feel like I was planted anywhere. It had become second nature for me to just throw my toothbrush into my carry-on bag and go. I was operating on autopilot, and I didn't care that I had been battling the flu with barely the strength to stand. I needed to get back to Ma.

The phone rang just as I was about to call the airline. It was the doctor.

"I'm so glad you called. My sister told me that my mother was hysterical again last night. Is the pneumonia back? Is she going to be okay?"

"I just examined her. Her lungs are stable. There was a little fluid still visible, but it's probably the fluid that was still resident when they did the procedure. I've prescribed some medication that will help to dissolve some of the fluid that's there. I also prescribed something to help with the anxiety and sleep. I'm going to monitor her very closely over the next forty-eight hours."

I felt the tension in my body lighten. "I was about to book a flight to come back to the hospital."

"Your mother is stable and your family is here. I can give you my direct number if you want to call me over the next forty-eight hours."

I looked over at my bag and closed my eyes, trying to decide if I should still go. I thought about it for a moment and remembered that I had the flu and that maybe going to the hospital and possibly contaminating Ma with my flu wasn't a good idea after all.

"Okay. Yes, please, I would like to stay in touch with you."

"Very well then. I'll have the nurse give you a call with my information and also ask them to keep you abreast."

When I hung up the phone, I didn't know whether to defy my own sense of clarity and hop the next plane to Columbia or just wait it out like the doctor suggested.

None of those options seemed that it would settle down my anxiety. So I picked up the phone and dialed Ma's room. When Eileen answered, I told her to put Ma on the phone.

I waited for a few minutes, listening to the muffled sounds before I finally heard Ma's weak and shallow voice. "Yeah?"

I closed my eyes and tried to find words that I thought would make her suddenly say: *You can come and sign me out of this hospital and take me home so I can fry you up some fish. I'm all better now.*

Instead I just started sobbing into the phone: "Ma, now I need you to stop all that talk about God taking you. It's up to you to get better, and you can't get better if you keep giving up hope. Please, Ma. Please don't say those words again. You need to be asking God to heal you instead of taking you. Please, Ma. We need you to get better. Please."

I heard her raspy breathing through the oxygen mask as I waited, just shut my mouth like Ma told me to do ever since I was a little girl. *You know, if you just close that mouth of yours sometimes and let someone get a word in edgewise, maybe you do yourself a favor.*

So I closed my mouth, hoping for her to get a word in edgewise, but still she said nothing. I imagined her with Eileen holding the phone to her ear, the mask on her face with her eyes closed.

"Alright, Ma? I know you're tired. I'll call you tomorrow, okay?"

Still she said nothing, and then I heard Eileen's voice on the other end.

"I guess Ma's tired. Let's let her get some rest, and I'll call you tomorrow."

I held on to the phone a little longer, wanting so desperately to hear Ma's voice again, wanting her to just say what I so desperately need to hear her say.

"How does she look?"

I heard Eileen take a deep breath. "She looks tired, really tired."

I forced back the tears that were building in my throat. "Alright then. I'll call her tomorrow."

I don't remember saying goodbye. I just remember hearing the dial tone and feeling so hopeless, so lost.

SNOW WHITE

There are moments in your life when you know that something beyond your understanding, your limited capabilities as a human being, is happening. But you must trust in the moment and be present to receive it.

I woke up the next morning feeling completely exhausted from a restless sleep and the flu. Everything ached: my body, my head, my heart. I dragged myself into the shower and just let the hot water wash away my misery. It was 7:00 a.m. and already I started planning my day before my bare feet set ground against the warmth of the bathmat that covered the concrete floor. The floor reminded me of what I was feeling at that moment—cold, hard, sad. I wrapped myself in my white terrycloth robe, and as much as I knew I needed to write, I didn't have the energy nor the creativity to meddle in my fictional characters' business today. I barely had enough strength to meddle in my own. For some reason, it didn't even occur to me to call the hospital. As I think about it now, I wondered why that wasn't the first thing on my mind when it had been the only thing that I'd thought about for the last several months.

I made my way to my office and forced myself to get caught up on Saving Promise. Lately, I questioned who was I really trying to *save*—me, Ma, or Promise. Today, I just didn't have the energy to save anyone, including myself. I still felt groggy from the Nyquil I had taken around midnight when I'd awoken in a cold sweat and fever, but I pushed through it. I didn't know how much time had passed, but at some point, I went into the kitchen to make some green tea when the phone rang.

I rushed to grab the phone when the caller ID announced the call was coming from South Carolina. It was John.

"You need to come back right away. The doctor told us we needed to consult with the hospital priest because she may not make it through the day."

I didn't know if it was the Nyquil that had my mind pulled into a stupor or my heart that felt a sudden crushing that halted my senses.

"*What?*"

"Your mother. The doctor said we need to gather the family and call the priest because she's not going to make it through the day."

"What do you mean *she's not going to make it through the day?* What day? Where's the doctor? I need to talk to him."

"He just left. I'll ask the nurse to have him call you."

I hung up the phone and rushed to my room and started putting on anything I could find. Then I looked for my purse with my wallet and ID. I was not thinking about what I was doing or how I was doing it. I just needed to get to Ma.

Just as I was about to grab the phone to call the airline, it rang.

"Your father told me you wanted to speak with me."

"Yes, doctor. My father said something about my mother not making it through the day. But when we spoke yesterday you said that when the fluid was drained from her lungs she was breathing better and we were going to monitor her condition for forty-eight hours. Didn't you? Didn't you say those words to me? So why are you calling the priest and talking about she may not make it through the day?"

I don't quite remember what he said next or how he said it. I just remember hanging up the phone and calling the airline to find out that the next available flight wouldn't be for a few hours.

"My mother's dying. She needs me. Please I need to get to Columbia, South Carolina, right away. Please."

"Ma'am, there's a flight that leaves about thirty minutes earlier than the other flights."

I didn't care that it was only thirty minutes; it was going to get me to Ma that much sooner. So I grabbed my coat and purse and drove frantically to the airport. When I walked up to the ticket desk, I didn't realize I was trembling with tears.

"My mother is sick, and I need to go to Columbia, South Carolina to be with her. The doctor called the priest and said we need to gather the family. She's dying. I need to get there. I need to see my mother. She can't die. Please help me get to my mother. Please."

The ticket agent reached for my hand and held it.

"Ma'am, I am so sorry about your mother. I am so very sorry. We are going to do everything we can to get you to your mother."

I couldn't stop trembling. I couldn't stop crying. I just stood there shaking and crying and babbling.

The ticket agent stood there awhile and let me cry. Then she kindly reached for the wallet in my hand and looked for my ID.

"We're going to get you to your mother. Your flight leaves in about an hour and the flight is only one hour and thirty minutes. We'll have you there in no time. You just hang on, okay?"

I shook my head. I couldn't speak anymore.

"You'll be departing from Gate C. Do you have any bags you need to check?"

"No, I didn't bring any bags. Just my purse."

"Alright. Now here's your boarding pass. Gate C is down the corridor that way." She handed me some tissues and pointed toward the gates.

"Thank you," I mouthed. Then I turned to walk toward the gates and for the first time, I noticed the mounds of people standing in line, staring at me, many with looks of sheer sorrow and compassion on their faces; others just wanted me to get moving so they could make their flights.

After I made my way through security and over to the gate, it was the longest wait of my life before I finally heard the flight agent announce that the flight to Columbia was ready to board. By then my frantic cry had tapered down to a soft sob.

I took my seat next to an elderly woman with snow-white hair and a round pleasant face. No sooner had the flight attendants started with the pre-flight safety demonstration than I closed my eyes and started praying. Praying like I had never prayed before. I needed God to hear me. I needed Him to just answer this one prayer for me, and I promised to do whatever He asked of me from now on. I told Him that I needed for Ma to live and it was up to Him now. "Please, God," I begged. "Please."

I had worked myself back into another frantic cry, unaware again of the people around me or the flight attendant who now scaled the aisle before we took off. My cries were not faint sobs that you try to suppress when you know people are watching or the quiet whimpering of distress, but the anguished wailing of a young cub grieving for her mother.

"Honey, what's wrong?"

I turned and looked at the white-haired woman next to me. My eyes were bloodshot from all the crying. My face was flush from the flu. And my hair and clothes looked disheveled because I'd thrown on the first thing I could find. It took me a little while to get past the sobs before I could speak. I told her everything about Ma, everything I had told God.

"If she dies, I don't know what I'm going to do. I can't live without my mother."

There are moments in your life when you know that something beyond your understanding, your limited capabilities as a human being, is happening. If I had a million words, still I would not be able to put it in a way that would make it believable.

She looked at me thoughtfully for a moment, then held out her hand, and for some reason, I took it.

"You need not worry, your mother is at peace now. You must be strong for her and for your family. God is going to answer your prayers. Just you wait and see."

I looked at her for a moment, considering her words, and solemnly nodded. Something about the way she spoke, the compassion in her eyes, calmed me. For the remainder of the flight, I sat there quietly, peering out the small window, looking at the beautiful blue-gray sky and fluffy white clouds. I was unusually calm sitting next to her.

After a while, once the flight attendant announced that we were preparing for landing, she spoke again. "You remember what I said. Your mother is at peace, and you need to be strong. She's going to be just fine."

She was silent again, and I began to think about what she said: *Ma was at peace. She was going to be just fine.* To me her words meant that Ma's pain would stop and she would pull through this. She was right, I thought. I needed to be strong to help Ma get better. She was going to be just fine.

Before I left, I turned to thank her, and she held my gaze and smiled.

"Remember what I told you."

I didn't have a smile in me to return, but what I did have now was a sheer sense of calm and gratitude that quickly carried me through the airport, past the baggage claim area, and outside where I looked for Anthony, whom I had called to pick me up.

I spotted him and his wife standing next to their car waiting for me.

I quickly made my way over to them. "How's Ma?"

Anthony's face turned down, then he looked away, and back at me. "She's gone. Ma's gone."

I looked at him, puzzled. *"What? What did you say?"*

Anthony reached for me and I knocked his hand away. "She's gone. Ma's gone."

I collapsed in Anthony's arms, the weight of my grief pulling me down.

I can't tell you how I ended up in the backseat of Anthony's car cradled in a fetal position. I just lay there sobbing. "I need to see her, Anthony. I need to see Ma." For some reason, I was still thinking if only I could see her, I could still save her. Once Ma sees me, she'll wake up, the same way she got up out of that bed the day I fried her some fish.

When we got to the hospital, I stood in the parking lot, looking up at the big white building. My legs felt like jelly.

"I can't go in there! I can't do it!"

Anthony pulled me in his arms and held me. Held me like I had never been held before.

"You gotta do it. You gotta come say goodbye to Ma."

I finally took Anthony's hand and let him lead me into the hospital and up to the familiar floor where I had spent so much time with Ma.

The moment we got off the elevator, I could hear people singing gospel music. There were so many people, our family, packed inside Ma's room, singing her favorite songs.

Aunt Deller and Uncle Bobby came into the hall where I stood unable to go inside.

"Aunt Deller, Ma's gone? Ma can't be gone!"

"She's gone, baby. But you come on in and say goodbye to her."

"I can't do it, Aunt Deller. I can't do it!"

My legs buckled and I went sliding to the floor. Uncle Bobby lifted me and sat me on a chair next to Ma's room.

"I can't breathe. I'm going to be sick. I have to throw up."

Aunt Deller held me in her arms until I calmed down.

"Now, baby, you got to come and say goodbye to your mother. She would want you to say goodbye to her. Now, come on in with me. She's resting peacefully and the family is here. You can do it."

For some reason I thought about Snow White—the elderly white-haired woman on the flight, what she said to me, and I suddenly got real still, listening to the gospel music floating from Ma's room. After a long while, Aunt Deller stood, took my hand, and slowly led me into the room.

Ma lay on the hospital bed, a white sheet folded at her chest, her eyes closed, her face tilted toward the ceiling.

I walked slowly up to the bed. Ma had been dead for less than an hour. She died just as my flight touched down. I felt my legs shaking again before I collapsed next to her, cradled my head into her still warm chest, and wept.

Wept until I could weep no more.

GRIEF

There is nothing that will break your heart more than losing someone you love.

M a's white casket sat at the center of the white church, surrounded by a rainbow of flowers as a sweet gospel voice
sang out high above the cathedral ceilings.

Why should I feel discouraged, why should the shadows come,
Why should my heart feel lonely, and long for heav'n and home,
When Jesus is my portion? My constant friend is He;
His eye is on the sparrow, and I know He watches me.

I sat there with the same calm that I had for the past week as I
planned Ma's funeral—the cream-laced dress she would wear, the
wig that framed her face perfectly, the pearl-studded earrings, the
custom gold ring that graced her right hand like a rainbow—one
colorful stone that marked the birth of each of her five children.

I sing because I'm happy, I sing because I'm free,
For His eye is on the sparrow, and I know He watches me.

I didn't remember much after leaving the hospital; just
remember waking up the next morning with a heaviness in my
heart. I would plan a home-going for Ma that I knew she would
be proud of.

Her funeral was to be held at the same church where she'd
held her own mother's funeral.

White flowers would grace the brass and white casket.

Beautiful photos of her celebrating life would be displayed.

The song that comforted her through the years would comfort her now.

And she would be laid to rest right next to her mother.

I didn't want my memories of Ma to be how she lived the last six months of her life. I wanted to remember the way her face lit up when she was surrounded by her children; how she adored John; the family gatherings, the vacations, the Sunday dinners; the way she cared for her grand and great-grandchildren; the way she held Promise at her first birthday.

Ma and little Promise on Promise's 1st birthday.
To view, visit: lymarlow.com/images

The calm faded within a few days after I started cleaning out Ma's bedroom—countless medicine bottles that covered her nightstand, the needles in the drawer, the head scarves scattered around the room. I wanted to touch her things once more, to smell her. I sniffed her clothes, the inside of her purse, her jewelry box. When I started cleaning the room, I saw Nancy sitting in the corner. I still part hated Nancy, but part of me was grateful to her. Nancy was a two-and-a-half-foot-tall oxygen tank that helped Ma breathe. I started to cry again, thinking about when I decided to give Nancy her name; the day we had brought Nancy home with us the first time Ma was released from the hospital. I lay on a blow-up bed in the living room outside Ma and John's bedroom in their temporary apartment. I hated listening to that thing night after countless night, the long breathing cord snaking its way from the living room into the bedroom to Ma's nostrils. The only way I could accept the fact that Ma could no longer breathe on her own was to give the oxygen tank a name.

"Stop calling that thing Nancy."

I smiled now just thinking about the way Ma said it, the way she looked at me like she had when I was that little seven-year-old girl who wanted nothing more than to be near her.

After I returned to my apartment, the first few weeks were unbearable. I'd lie awake most nights with an emptiness, listening to the river and the thoughts that kept me from sleep—*What if I had never taken Ma to Houston? What if I didn't leave the hospital to go home?*

Each morning, I'd drag myself out of bed, open my laptop, and just stare at it, just stare at it, trying so desperately to muster up the energy to do what I'd promised Ma I would do.

Heartbroken, I'd march back into my bedroom, undress, wrap myself back up in my blankets, and sleep. I didn't want to eat. I didn't want to think. I didn't want to live. Not without Ma.

I hated *Grief.*

Grief pulled me into a dark, dark place and snapped me like a twig. There were days when I just curled into the fetal position and cried, and nights when *Grief* ripped me from what little sleep I was getting and reminded me of what I *would've, should've, could've* done. *Grief* made me walk into the grocery store, the bank, Target, Walmart, and break down. *Grief* told me it was my fault that Ma was gone. *Grief* would knock me down one day and pick me up the next, telling me that it was okay to let it go. *Just let it go, Grief* encouraged. *Let it go.*

And I did. I tried to face *Grief* with the same conviction and courage I saw Ma face every day of her life. But my weak, pathetic spirit was no match for Ma's. First, I couldn't stand the sight of anything that was amiss in my perfect little world. Second, unlike Ma, I didn't know the meaning of *unconditional.* Ma liked, loved, and lived unconditionally. But everything I encountered, every move I made, every step I took was deliberate, like the programming language I learned in undergrad school, COBOL, with its structure and rules. And aside from occasionally attending church with Ma, I never talked to God. I would mumble grace before I ate most times and say the Lord's Prayer occasionally before I went to sleep, but rarely had I ever had a heart-to-heart with God. I tried a few times, but it always felt awkward, like I had suddenly decided to say hello to someone I'd been hiding from for a long time. In fact, I'd only recently learned to talk to God when Ma got sick. Then after I thought He took Ma from us, I questioned whether I could ever trust God again.

Now *Grief* was the closest thing I had to a God.

I could talk to *Grief* because *Grief* didn't make no bones about her intent. She haunted me like a plague, made sure that I was going to deal with her, whether I wanted to or not.

I haaattteeed *Grief!* Flat out hated, hated, hated her! And every day *Grief* and I went through the same routine: I'd drag out of bed, drop to my knees, beg for mercy, and draw on what little strength I had.

Drag. Drop. Draw.

Drag. Drop. Draw.

Drag. Drop. Draw.

Until finally, I called Sharon, my best friend in Philadelphia whom I'd been talking to almost daily, and when she heard my voice this time, she said, "I'm coming." That weekend, she drove three hours from Philadelphia to my apartment.

"You're going to get through this. You gotta be strong for your daughter and Promise, for your family," she kept saying. "I'm so proud of everything you're doing, and your mother is proud of you too. You gotta find the strength to go on. You can do it, Weezy!"

Weezy. That's what she'd been calling me for more than twenty-five years, ever since we first met and became friends through my then new job as the administrative assistant to the executive director for a nonprofit organization.

Weezy, the abused young mother who was determined to make something of her life. Now, I questioned who I really was—the little girl who thought she could twirl into Wonder Woman and fix the world? Weezy, who had overcome poverty, teen pregnancy, and abuse? Or the person who had transformed her life into the woman that Ma said she was proud of?

I wanted to believe I was all of them. But more than that, I wanted so desperately to be that woman who made Ma that promise.

I needed to be her. I so desperately needed her.

"Okay," I finally said to Sharon. "You're right. I need to do it—for Ma. I'll do it. I'll do it," I kept repeating, tears running down my face with *Grief* stalking me.

The following Monday after Sharon left, I dragged myself out of bed, made my way into my office, and willed myself to *do it for Ma.* Every day, I faced the day with the same intent: *to do it for Ma.* And that's what I did each day, like a toddler who's learning to put one foot in front of the other, slowly wobbling on chubby ankles until my balance faltered, and reaching to grab anything within arm's length to catch me: *Sleep, Prayer, Will.*

Within the first few months, I'd wobbled enough until I found myself on an Amtrak train out of New York City's Penn Station headed back to Washington DC. I had spoken about my family's story and domestic violence at an event in New York, and I was surviving on borrowed energy, along with a fake smile and a face that said everything was okay, but I was a complete mess!

I had not only just lost Ma, but I was also going through the divorce. Fortunately, it did not get ugly because all I wanted was out. I had also just decided to walk away from my career after IBM announced another round of layoffs and handed me the courage to dedicate my life to Saving Promise. I had already liquidated my retirement, my lifetime savings, and depleted and sold just about anything I owned of value. And it didn't help that I still had virtually no help after my team quit on me. So even though I would show up at an event or a meeting or take a call, I put my best face and voice forward, but inside I was dying.

I sat on that Amtrak train having one of the ugliest cries I'd had in public. Anyone would be ashamed to be exposed like that, but I didn't care. After breaking down in Walmart and Target, I had long since stopped caring about what other people thought, and I didn't try to hide it.

At some point, I reached down into my purse to grab my phone to call my daughter. She had been on speed dial because I needed to hear her voice, to be reminded of the promise I made to Ma.

"Mom, hold on," she said the moment she heard my voice. I heard her put the phone down and rustle off somewhere. It was midnight, and I imagined that I'd awakened her, I was sure of it. And I pretty much had an idea of what she was doing. My suspicions were confirmed when I heard three-year-old Promise's voice on the other end of the line.

"Bumble Bee, are you crying?"

Promise had started calling me Bumble Bee the time I'd taken her out for her first Halloween and my daughter had found the cutest bumblebee costume for her. She was only a year old, and when we'd walk up to the door and someone answered, I'd speak for Promise: *"I'm a bumblebee,"* I would say and stretch out the pumpkin basket for her treat. Ever since then, Promise called me Bumble Bee because she thought I was saying that *my* name was Bumble Bee.

"Yes, I'm crying," I said, unable to control the tears.

There was silence, and I heard her sigh as though she was thinking real hard. Then suddenly, I heard her little voice say: "But, Bumble Bee, just don't look at the monster."

Here was little Promise giving me back the same wisdom I'd given her when she was two years old. *Just close your eyes real tight and just don't look at the monster,* I had told her. My heart quickened at what I didn't know and would soon learn: this was just the beginning of the monsters that were still to come.

PART 2

THE LESSONS

"I think you have to know who you are.
Get to know the monster that lives in your soul,
dive deep into your soul and explore it."
–Tori Amos

It's Frightening

If someone had told me that my greatest lessons would come from my *monsters*, I would have roared a defiant: *Yeah, right!* But as I look back on my life, it is nothing short of remarkable how those frightening moments forced me to dive deep into my soul and explore who I really am.

THE SUNSHINE LADY

I'd had a pointy arrow pierced through my heart, been knocked square on my butt time and again, and had to muster the courage to get out of bed, but nothing had prepared me for what this woman said to me . . .

H*ush. Hush. Hush.*

That's what I told myself every day I woke up with my heart pained. Other than the times I sat on a padded steel table in an exam room with a stethoscope against my chest, I rarely noticed this complex muscular thing about the size of my closed fist. Now, I felt it every waking moment pulsing through me—*bop bop—bop bop—bop bop*—reminding me of just how very broken it was, *I was.*

Little by little, I began pacing and peddling and pushing my way back into my *new* normal. I had hired an intern, a twenty-something fresh out of grad school who had some gutsy ideas about how she could help me pick up the pieces.

The *pieces.*

I don't think she understood that she was going to earn that $10 an hour ten times over. And not because I'd planned to work her beyond her capable and overzealous eagerness, but because the *pieces* were scattered about like jacks.

Within a few weeks, *Twenty-something* and I propelled full steam ahead. First, I contracted one of my girlfriends—whom I thought was one of the most brilliant women I knew on the planet earth—to help me craft a plan to build Saving Promise while I prepared for the rerelease of my book *Color Me Butterfly* as part of a three-book deal I had just signed with Random House. I also hired a development director named Sylvia to help raise funds. The moment I met Sylvia, I felt a connection with her. Not only did she have a warm spirit, something I so desperately needed, but she also *got* my vision right away. It also helped that she had twenty-five years of experience managing and raising funds for nonprofits. I appealed to her heart as a leader, a visionary, a *woman*.

"I know you can't pay me what I typically earn, but I believe in you, L.Y., and I want to help you."

I'd always had a sixth sense about women—a sort of *it-takes-a-village-to-raise-a-child* mentality. At that moment, Saving Promise was the child, and women like Sylvia were my village.

I needed Sylvia and I got the sense that she needed me too. So I liquidated what little savings I had left to pay her and also to secure a public relations firm to launch a national domestic violence public awareness tour entitled *Saving Promise Comes to You*.

I felt like a big throbbing heart with legs that was just bopping along, trying desperately to hide from *Grief*. But I knew I needed to find the strength to do what Ma had told me to do.

So I buried my broken heart by working harder. My days had turned into an endless string of long hours, and my nights were sleepless for fear I wouldn't have the strength to get back up the next morning. I was feverishly working myself into a deep ditch, and it wouldn't be long before I would crash.

It was a Saturday morning, after yet another sleepless night when the phone rang. It was Sylvia.

"Doris Buffett is going to be signing her new book, *Giving It All Away*, today at a bookstore in Fredericksburg, Virginia. I think you should go to the book signing and tell her about Saving Promise."

Doris Buffett, the sister of billionaire Warren Buffett, and the founder of the Sunshine Lady Foundation, which helps educate battered and abused women—writes in her book about growing up the victim of her own mother's emotionally abusive rage and how her personal experiences have opened her heart to help others.

Until then, I had only heard of Warren Buffett and had little knowledge of his sister, Doris. But the moment I researched Ms. Buffett, I knew there was something special about her. She wasn't just a wealthy philanthropist who was far removed from the *real* society. She understood what it was like to be abused, live in poverty, and pull herself up by her bootstraps.

Less the billionaire part, I got Ms. Buffett, and I knew she would get me too! So it took me no time to shower, dress, and jump in my car to drive the nearly three hours to Fredericksburg.

On the drive there I practiced what I would say to her. I didn't want to flat out ask her for money, although I desperately needed it. I had liquidated all of my accounts, and I barely had enough money left to pay my rent. In fact, I was ashamed to admit to Sylvia that I couldn't go to the book signing because I hardly had enough money to pay for the gas, let alone buy the book. "Don't worry about that. I'll call the bookstore and pay for them to hold two copies for you. All you need to do is find a way to get there."

Sylvia's kindness made me weep.

It was the first time I had cried in front of anyone connected to Saving Promise. It was a side of me that I refused to let anyone see for fear they would pity me, and I didn't want that. Pity would send me crawling back to bed.

Fredericksburg, positioned midway between Washington DC and Richmond, Virginia, is a quaint historic town with streets lined by antique, specialty, and craft shops in eighteenth- and nineteenth-century buildings restored to pristine condition, museums, historical sites, and natural parks on both sides of the Rappahannock River, home to four Civil War battlefields and Doris Buffett.

The moment I stepped foot in this whimsical place I could see the irony. Behind the charm was a town where the Civil War had resulted in slaughter and bloody struggle. And I was not only knee-deep in American tragedy, but today was also the ninth anniversary of 9/11. I tried to shake off a feeling of dread.

I parked a few blocks from where the book signing was being held and sat in my car, waiting. I wasn't ready to go inside yet because I had cried nearly the whole way there, thinking about Ma and the state of Saving Promise and Sylvia, who had to pay for the books I couldn't afford, *and* the fact that I was about to meet a woman who happened to be the sister of one of the wealthiest men in the world.

After a while, I cleaned my face, put on some makeup, and finally made my way to the bookstore. The moment I stepped inside, I spotted Ms. Buffett sitting next to a man who I would later learn was Michael Zitz, the author. I tried not to stare at her, but I couldn't help it. She looked so regal, so approachable with her fluffy white hair perfectly encasing her charming face and eyes.

There was a line of people waiting for their books to be signed as I made my way over to the counter to pick up my books.

"My name is L.Y. Marlow. I believe you have some books for me."

"Oh yes. A nice lady called it in and paid for them. She told me to tell you to be sure to get a copy signed for her too."

She smiled and handed the books to me with a receipt. I tried to smile back, but suddenly, I felt lightheaded and quickly made my way out of the store, crossed the street, and pulled my cell phone out of my purse to call Sharon.

"I came to Fredericksburg to meet Doris Buffett, who's signing her new book, and I can't do it. I can't do it!" I babbled into the phone the moment I heard Sharon's voice on the other end. When I was done telling her the whole story, including the part about not having enough money to buy the books and running out of the bookstore like a weirdo, Sharon got real quiet for a moment. Then she said, "Weezy, you pull yourself together and go back to that bookstore!"

By now, I was crying so hard that a woman and man who were walking by stopped and asked me if I was okay. I nodded with the phone still pressed against my ear as she reached inside her purse for some tissue and handed it to me.

"Are you sure you're okay?"

I nodded again and watched the couple walk away, suddenly embarrassed about standing on a street corner in Fredericksburg, Virginia, having an emotional breakdown.

"Weezy, you've gotta pull yourself together!" Sharon said again. "You've come too far to turn back now. You go back in there and call me when you're done. I'm gonna wait for your call."

I straightened up and wiped my face. I knew I would hate myself if I walked away from a once-in-a-lifetime opportunity. What were the chances I would ever have that kind of access to a Buffett again?

"Okay. I can do this. I can."

As I approached the store, I paused several times to take a deep breath and tried to force myself not to think about the things that were going through my mind—*What would I say to her? Why couldn't I just pull it together? What the hell was I doing?*

My legs trembled as I stepped inside and looked over at the table where Ms. Buffett was signing a book for a woman who stood smiling down at her. There was now only one other person waiting in line, and I slowly made my way over there to stand behind her.

When the woman in front of me walked away, I stepped up to the table, and before I knew it, my whole body started trembling and a river of tears slid down my face, and I broke down.

I mean, *broke down!*

"Ms. Buffett, my mother died and I come from a family of four generations of domestic violence, and my daughter is still in an abusive relationship and I worry about Promise because now she's a victim and I have an organization called Saving Promise and I gave up my career and I don't have any money left to keep the organization going and I don't even have anything left to survive and I . . ."

Michael Zitz stood up, possibly to protect Ms. Buffett from this deranged woman who stood there trembling and crying and babbling like a maniac.

Ms. Buffett put up her hand to Michael. "No leave her. She's fine."

"I'm sorry. I'm so sorry. I didn't mean to do this. I'm so sorry, Ms. Buffett."

"You come sit next to me and talk to me. Michael let her have your seat."

I took the seat next to her. She handed me a tissue and let me cry a little longer, and after I blew my nose, she said, "What's your name?"

"Lydia."

"Now, Lydia, you tell me what's wrong."

Suddenly, I felt a sense of calm come over me the same way it had when I sat next to Snow White on the flight. I wiped my face and took a deep breath and slowly began to tell her everything: about how Ma had suddenly gotten sick and how I had to take care of her and how she had died; about my family history of domestic violence and the terrible abuse my grandmother, Ma, me, and my daughter suffered; about Promise and how I started Saving Promise and had invested everything I owned and how I barely had enough left to keep the organization going; and finally about the public awareness tour.

"How is your daughter and Promise now?"

I said something that I had learned to say after realizing that I needed to find a way to come to terms with the terrible situation that my daughter and Promise was still in. I said, *Today they are fine.*

Ms. Buffett then told me her story of growing up in an abusive situation with her mother and about her foundation and how they help woman and children like my daughter and Promise. She asked if my daughter was in school, and I told her that she had gone to the University of Maryland and that she was now working and had a decent job.

"Do you have a proposal about your organization and the tour?"

"Yes, I do," I blurted this out without thinking. I had no more of a proposal than I had control of my emotional breakdown. But I would have said that I'd flown a 747 jet if she asked me.

She took out a piece of paper and wrote down the name of the lady who ran her nonprofit. "You give her a call on Monday, and you tell her you spoke to me and that I told you to contact her, and then I want you to send her your proposal. And you tell her I told you to call her. You say it just like that."

I nodded. She hugged me before I stood up.

"Would you like us to sign your books?"

I nodded again and handed the books to her.

Giving It All Away
THE DORIS BUFFETT STORY
TO LYDA,
ALL THE BEST!

MICHAEL ZITZ

I'm glad we met— We have
a lot in common—
with best wishes,
Doris Buffett

Doris Buffett and Michael Zitz sign my copy of Giving It All Away;
Fredericksburg Art Museum Store, Fredericksburg, VA, September 11, 2010.

When I got back to my car, I called Sharon first and then Sylvia.

"She's going to be at the Border's Bookstore in Stafford, Virginia, tomorrow. You should take the proposal up there and hand-deliver it to her," Sylvia suggested.

"You think so?" I asked, a question that was out of the ordinary for me. Before Ma passed away that would naturally have been the first thought to come to my mind. In fact, by the time I'd planned to meet Ms. Buffett, I would have figured out what she liked for breakfast and taken it to her.

I drove home and stayed up most of the night writing the proposal, and the next morning I drove the two hours to Stafford. I'd arrived an hour early and parked my car at the far end of the shopping center and waited until it was time to go in.

Convinced that I *was* not going to cry again, this time when I walked into Borders and saw Ms. Buffett sitting next to Michael Zitz, I turned in the opposite direction, down an aisle, and stood behind an island of books, watching her.

I had cried so much the day before that I didn't think I had any moisture left in my body. But my knees started trembling, my stomach started doing somersaults, and my face twitched like it was ready for a slide of tears as I lurked behind rows of books, stalking Doris Buffett.

I stayed in that aisle until I got my legs back, and then I slowly made my way over to her table.

Her face lit up when she saw me. "Lydia, what are you doing here?"

I felt a little embarrassed. "Well, Ms. Buffett, yesterday you told me to send my proposal to your executive director, and I thought I should hand deliver it to you."

"You didn't need to do that."

"I know, but I just wanted to make sure you got it."

"Well, that was very thoughtful of you. I will be sure to read it, and I want you to still send it to the address that I gave you."

I stood there, not yet ready to leave her. "Alright then. I'm leaving now."

Part of me half expected her to say, *No, don't go. Stay awhile. Let's talk again.* And part of me knew that if I stayed any longer, it would get weird. So I walked away.

On Monday morning, I looked up the address to the Sunshine Lady Foundation, mailed a copy of the proposal, and then I followed up with a call. The first time I called, there was no answer so I left a message explaining my encounter with Ms. Buffett. I waited until the next day before I tried again. This time, someone did answer and I explained why I'd called and asked to speak to the woman that Ms. Buffett had written down. "She's not available right now. I'll give her the message and ask her to return your call." I hung up, expecting that my call would be returned that afternoon.

The next morning and the morning after that and the morning after that, I waited for her call. For nearly two weeks,

I called and left messages until finally my caller ID announced the call I'd been waiting for. When the woman on the other end introduced herself, I lunged into the whole story: about my meetings with Ms. Buffett and the proposal I'd taken to her and had also mailed and how she said she wanted to help, and then after explaining everything, I ended it with what Ms. Buffett told me to say: *She wanted me to let you know that she asked me to call you.*

I'd had a pointy arrow pierced through my heart, had been knocked square on my butt time and again, and had to muster the courage to get out of bed, but nothing had prepared me for what this woman said to me: "Ms. Buffett is eighty-two years old and she doesn't remember half the things she promises to people. By now, she probably doesn't even remember your name. So I wouldn't get my hopes up if I were you. We'll take a look at your proposal, and if it fits our program, we'll be in touch."

Other than receiving a newsletter from the Sunshine Lady Foundation, I never heard from her or Ms. Buffett again. It was the day that my resolve diminished, and I began to lose hope in my dream, in myself, in Saving Promise.

THE TOUR, THANKSGIVING
& THE BALLOON

Life is a tour. Every place, every stop, every moment is about discovering who you really are and getting to your destination. Though often painful, it is so very worth the journey.

I vividly recall the day I made the decision that if I was going to take on this global crisis, I needed to stand in my truth and own it—I mean *really* own it. But standing in my truth brought me face to face with *Despair*. The more *Despair* whispered in my ear, the more I was reminded about *Grief*, the challenges that I'd faced, *not to get my hopes up*. But *Despair* also brought moments of spiritual enlightenment. I took comfort in knowing that my grandmother Mama, Ma, me, my daughter, and Promise and the countless women and children who were victims of domestic violence needed a voice, and if I was going to be that *voice*, I would have to raise it and raise it loud. What better way to do that, I thought, than to launch a public awareness tour targeting some of the most visible cities in the country—New York, Chicago, Houston, Philadelphia—and tell them my story? And not just in any place, but in a place that could potentially put me in front of millions of people.

The mall.

We targeted some of the largest malls we could find during the busiest season of the year.

For ten weekends straight, we went to a different mall in a different city, and I'd stand there in my purple shirt (the color of the domestic violence movement) and read an excerpt from *Color Me Butterfly*, shouting at the top of my lungs. Sometimes, people would stop to listen, and other times they'd just whisk by as if I wasn't standing there at all.

Wolfchase Galleria Mall, October 10, 2010, Memphis, Tennessee
To view, visit: lymarlow.com/images

Secretly, I abhorred it. To begin with, I'd always been a closeted introvert who got grasshoppers in my stomach, ready to vomit at the thought of opening my mouth. But then ask that closeted introvert to stand in front of thousands of people in a mall and air her dirty laundry, that would be patently insane. There were some weekends *Twenty-something* had to coax me out of the hotel bed. It was the hardest thing I had ever had to do. Especially during those times when women would confide in me about their own stories. It was difficult to listen to so many terrible, terrible stories like the time one woman told me about how her husband had beaten her so badly that she'd nearly died, and another whose boyfriend had strangled her until she was unconscious, and another who'd had to flee her home with her children because her husband had threatened to kill her and the children.

Once, while in Philadelphia, a woman came up to me and told me that her boyfriend was stalking her at that very moment. "See, he's threatening to kill me." She pulled out her cell phone and showed me the ominous text. "You have to call the police!" I insisted. I quickly told *Twenty-something* about the situation, and we flagged down a security guard, who helped us contact the police. Once the police came and we got her to safety, the fullness of it welled up inside of me. I could barely get out of bed and women were looking to *me* to save them.

Every city, every mall, every story was taking its toll on me.

By the time we got to our second to last city on the tour, I was so run down that the nostalgia of returning to Houston since Ma had died never crossed my mind. The memories wouldn't hit me until I found myself walking through the airport, driving on the freeway, passing by the familiar places. That night while in the hotel room that I shared with *Twenty-something* (I didn't have enough money to afford separate rooms), I got in my bed, turned my back to her, and sobbed into my pillow.

The tour ended the week before Thanksgiving, and I went to Lugoff to spend the holiday with John, Treasure, and Promise. We had cooked all the same foods Ma had cooked, baked all the pies and cakes she'd baked, but it just wasn't the same. The reality of having Thanksgiving without Ma sat on our faces like old makeup. Somehow I had this crazy thought that by trying to mimic Ma in the kitchen, I could make our pain go away.

There were times when I would be alone sitting on my sofa or at my desk or lying in my bed and I'd feel this overwhelming presence of her. The first time it happened, it frightened me. Then I read somewhere that you should feel comforted by these visits, so I started talking to Ma, about *everything*. I'd be in the shower and have a thought, and I'd share it with her; or I'd be wrestling with a decision about Saving Promise and I'd ask her opinion; or I'd be frustrated with my daughter and I'd say, *Ma, I know you told me to be patient with her, but I'm gonna kill her!*

But that evening we didn't talk about Ma. Not because we wanted to deny *Grief,* but talking about her would crumble us all.

How strange it was not to see Ma in the kitchen, fussing over a pot of greens or checking the turkey in the oven. Everything I was accustomed to since I was a child was gone. So we just ate Thanksgiving dinner then retreated to our rooms.

Treasure and I sat on the bed in the guest room talking and had not noticed when Promise had wandered into the living room until sometime later when we heard her giggling.

"Who is she talking to out there?"

Treasure shrugged, and I followed her out into the living room to check.

Promise stood there holding a helium balloon of Dora the Explorer, which had floated to the eighteen-foot-high cathedral ceiling during our last visit months before when it had slipped from her hand.

"How did you get that balloon?"

Promise looked up at her mother, smiling. "Nana gave it to me."

Treasure and I both looked up at the ceiling and then at each other. In that moment, we were without words. We were without reason. We were without a lot of things, except for Ma.

She was, as I always suspected, there with us.

MARCH 9TH

Every soul on the planet earth has a place and a time. Life is not for our living, but for the living of a higher purpose.

For more than a year, I'd been attending St. John Baptist Church, a small church not too far from where I lived. The first time I'd visited and heard the pastor preach a sermon that seemed intended *only* for me, I'd cried so hard thinking about all the terrible things that had happened in my life: losing Ma, another divorce, my dwindling bank account, going back and forth to Lugoff to now care for John, who was having health issues, and Saving Promise.

Never before had I ever seriously thought about running back to IBM and begging them to give me back my job. It was all too much, especially after both *Twenty-something* and Sylvia left.

I was devastated.

I trusted them, believed that they *believed* in me. So less than a year later when Sylvia submitted her resignation citing that she found another opportunity and couldn't work with me anymore because I couldn't afford to pay her what she was worth, I resented her.

Yes, *resented* her. Partly because I questioned if she ever really believed in me or if I was nothing more than a transition paycheck until she found a better paying job. I'd liquidated all the funds I had left and invested in her, believing she would help me raise more funds. So when she just left without having raised a cent and knowing that I was running out of money, I felt like she twisted the knife that was still lodged in my heart.

A month later, *Twenty-something* left too. I didn't resent her in the way I resented Sylvia. In fact, when *Twenty-something* told me she wanted to leave (even though I had appealed to her to stay), I offered to pay her for a month after she resigned so she could look for another job. But again I felt like what little village I had had abandoned me.

Besides which, I was tired of receiving rejection letter after rejection letter from the countless agencies, foundations, and people I'd reached out to for help. I felt hopeless.

Most mornings I lay in bed asking, *Why? For what?*

God knows I tried every single day to get up and get me some hope. But when Ma died, a part of me and my passion for Saving Promise died too. On occasion, I had thought about calling the pastor, but I was too embarrassed to tell him why I had not joined his church. It wasn't that I didn't have a special place in my heart for God. I just didn't believe in the need to join a church when churches seemed to have more mayhem and madness than I had in my own life.

Things got really bad one day when I was finalizing Ma's estate and noticed her death certificate. I didn't know what a death certificate looked like until I received Ma's in the mail. There it was in a plain white envelope huddled amongst the junk mail, as if Ma were no more valuable than the thirty-four cent stamp that got it there.

This greenish official-looking document narrowed Ma's life down to the date of her death, *March 9, 2010.* I'd seen that date many times, but for some reason this time it stayed with me. For the next few weeks, I couldn't shake why the date stalked me like *Grief* and *Despair* until one morning it hit me!

I got up and quickly tore through my files looking for Ma's and Daddy's death certificates. Then right there before my very eyes was the answer: Ma and Daddy had died on the same day, *March 9th*, nearly forty years apart.

For the next few days, I walked around in a daze, telling no one, afraid to say it out loud as if by speaking it into being would make it more *real*. And I wasn't ready for it to be real. *Real* meant that I would have to own up to all that I thought was true about life and death and God; that God was beyond my limited, diluted understanding; that maybe every soul on the planet earth has a place and a time; that life was not for our living, but for the living of a higher purpose; that perhaps my place and time and purpose had already been decided, and there was nothing I could do about it.

I don't remember at what point I started to pray like I had never prayed before. I'd fold down on my knees in my living room, hands clasped against my forehead, and prance around a prayer as though the God I was now talking to was different.

Father, give me the strength to do your will, have your way with me.

That's how I now ended my prayers, unsure of what I was asking for.

Soon after, I was invited to a national faith conference to deliver a workshop at a church in Washington DC. Pastors from every denomination were coming together to talk about addressing domestic violence in the church. While I had spoken at many churches before now, there was something different about this time.

The morning of the conference, I sat in the front pew mesmerized by a purple cross that hung behind the church's podium as a statuesque domestic violence advocate and faith leader with a deep booming voice, belted out a sermon that electrified my soul.

As I stared at that cross, a feeling washed over me; it was the same feeling that I got as a child when I watched Ma get the Holy Ghost. Perhaps it was because the color purple symbolizes the domestic violence movement or because the cross symbolizes faith or because of my prayers. Deep in my soul I *knew* the pastor's words and the purple cross were signs that my life was no longer my own and that God was about to have his way with me.

MA AND A MAN

If we want to experience true intimacy, we need to be taught to love aspects of ourselves—again and again—by the people around us.

—Ken Page, *LSCW, Psychology Today,*
"How to Love Yourself First"

While there were a lot of things I had to come to learn to live with, there were two things I didn't know how to live without: Ma and a man.

That proverbial nonsense about learning to love yourself first had nothing to do with me. At least that's what I'd convinced myself when it came to men. Hadn't God created Adam and Eve? Wasn't it customary for a woman to want to have a man? Weren't we supposed to have a family to be happy?

Since the time I was old enough to take a liking to boys, I had developed this insatiable need to always have a boy near me, around me, a part of me. I liked everything there was to like about a boy. The way he walked, the way he talked, the way he smelled—even if stinky at times. I would spend hours with my Barbie and Ken dolls planning the wedding, the house, the babies. Barbie was this ambitious woman who could do it all—have a great career, be a good wife, and be a good friend to her other Barbies all the while carting her little Barbies to soccer practice, piano lessons, and PTA meetings. There wasn't a meal, cake, or dress that Barbie couldn't make or bake. And Barbie worshipped Ken. His energy, the sporty car he drove, and his dirty drawers.

I believed in Adam and Eve. I believed in Barbie and Ken. I believed in *love*.

But in the time since I had separated from my third husband, I had discovered that I was no longer a slave to love. Within two years of leaving my husband, I'd come to appreciate how to sleep in *my* own bed, to find comfort in *my* own warmth, to breathe *my* own air. But I'd be dishonest if I said that walking away from my marriage was easy.

The day we had gone to court to finalize our divorce, I sat next to my ex-husband-to-be watching countless couples on opposite sides of the courtroom immersed in their divided animosity and anger, wanting nothing more than to be as far removed from the person that they once couldn't stand to live without. We, unlike so many other couples, sat together as I listened to him express his regrets for not working harder to save our marriage.

When the judge finally asked us to approach the bench, we stood on opposite sides of the courtroom as he read through similar language that we heard him read to the countless couples that had come before us: "You have been separated for at least a year; you have community property and assets that needs to be dissolved equitably; this is an uncontested no-fault divorce."

No fault?

What did that mean anyway? Weren't we there because one or both of us were at fault? The same *fault* that I suspected Ma had meant when she told me that it takes two to tango.

It is that *tango* that has often gotten me twisted up in a mass of confusion and mess.

I answered the judge's questions: *yes,* I understood that it was a no fault divorce; *yes,* we have been separated for at least a year; *yes,* we have community property; *yes,* I was sure that I wanted to give up all rights to any property, assets, and alimony. The only thing I wanted was to leave the marriage as quietly and humanely as we'd entered into it.

"Very well, then." I watched the judge write something down and hand it to the bailiff. "You will receive your divorce decree in the mail within sixty days. You are free to go."

Free to go?

What had taken years of courting, cultivating, and compromising was dissolved in less than five minutes. Now, I was free, I was alone, and I was *lonely.*

Lonely told me that it was not okay to feel this way, that I didn't *need* a man but that I deserved one. But walking away from a loveless marriage left me no desire to get tangoed up again. Nor was I ready to give up this newfound freedom and *woman* I had discovered. Given the number of failed relationships, I was no longer wedded to the idea of marriage or a soul mate. The marriage and the soul were on hold. Now I was in search of a partner.

Partner?

What the hell did that mean anyway? This newfound word that suddenly showed up in the same way cell phones had showed up and consumed our lives. A partner to me was like a cell phone plan: we get to pick the phone we can afford, the features, and how many minutes we will invest, and if we should decide to cancel the contract, there's a fair penalty—meaning just give me back my shit and you take your shit—then we can walk away.

With a *partner* in mind, I had turned to the only logical place to find him: *online dating.*

Never before had I dared to go online in search of a man. I'd heard all kinds of horrible stories that made me believe that only *desperate* women went online to meet men. Was I now one of those *desperate* women? And was it even discreet or safe? I'd pondered these thoughts for days until *Lonely* convinced me that for every one bad story there were two good stories from women who swore by online dating. I was part intimidated and part exhilarated, and I had nothing to lose.

Being analytical and sometimes overly meticulous, I did my homework and even called up the site that I'd chosen and asked so many questions you would have thought I was interviewing them for a job at the White House. In a way, I *was.* My *White House* was my fragile and sacred heart and home.

The first time I went on the site, I sat in my living room with a glass of red wine and my laptop, filling out a profile that took me three hours to complete. Then for the next few weeks, I'd reviewed several profiles before I found him. There he was, gift-wrapped in words that spoke to me. *Divorced. A father who adored his two grown daughters. Career-minded. Compassionate. Caring. Honest.*

Lonely screamed: *It's him! Your partner!*

I started typing a message then suddenly stopped. *Are you sure you're ready for this?*

Lonely intervened. *Of course you are! You deserve a partner, remember?*

I tried to decide if I should send the message or not. I was tired of screwing it up, but I was also heartsick. So I crafted a long message about how his words spoke to me, and before I could talk myself out of it again, I quickly hit the SEND button, shut down my laptop, and went to bed.

The next morning when I logged on to the site and saw that I had a message from him, my heart leaped. I was nervous about opening it. For one, I'd tossed and turned all night, drumming up this fairytale story about what he thought about my message, how he would respond, and where we would meet for our first date. By the time I finally drifted off, I was hopelessly tangled up again.

I could feel my heart smile as I sat cuddled with my laptop against the backdrop of my bedroom that had for months been comforting me like a giant slumbering sack. With the sun rising, tempered against my window, I devoured his every word before I finally heard *Lonely* say:

Go get 'em!

STAPLES

No longer was I a woman who did not know who she was. There was a conviction in me, despite the fact that I had to staple my heart, my home, a man, and my coat.

The three weeks I spent with Tate on the dating site exchanging thought-provoking revelations followed by late-night phone calls that lingered into the wee hours of the morning made me feel alive again.

By the time we decided to meet, I desperately wanted to feel and look like a woman who was confident, self-assured, and sexy. Not the woman who was huddled on her knees, clinging to *Grief, Despair,* and *Lonely,* daily drowning in her own tears.

For our first date, I'd spent hours trying to decide what to wear and finally settled on a pair of jeans, black sweater, a black leather jacket, and short-heeled burgundy leather boots. We met at a quaint wine café only blocks away from my home. Tate was every bit of what I had imagined: kind, compassionate, caring, and very handsome. We drank a bottle of my favorite wine and talked again for hours about everything—our past, our future, our dreams. I liked that he had spent nearly thirty years in the military and had an uncanny discipline and discernment; that he had been married for more than twenty-five years and took care of his family and was still very close to his daughters; and that we shared a love of wine and music and good food. I especially liked his confidence and the way he didn't shy away from the tough questions.

When Tate walked me to my car, he kissed me so passionately that I thought my heart would explode. Just blow up right there in a million tiny pieces. Then he told me that he wanted to share his life with someone he could grow with.

Grow. That's what I wanted, too. To grow beyond the frail, heartbroken woman I'd grown into over the past year.

Coincidentally, Tate lived only ten minutes from me so we started seeing each other a few times a week and spending weekends together. At some point, I'd written a letter confessing that while I had dated a few men since my divorce, he was the first one that I felt an immediate connection to—a letter that led to Tate moving in with me within three months. We had gone shopping together to buy a new bedroom set. We had painted the walls soft bold colors and bought new pots and pans. We had even bought a beautiful floor fountain with water cascading over tumbled stones to create an oasis of peace, calm, and tranquility, something that I so desperately craved.

While Tate and I were setting up *house*, I was also trying to secure Saving Promise. I had recruited a new board to help me raise funds and had written letters telling my story to people of influence, including twelve congress men and women. I was elated when I'd received a response from more than half and one that had invited me to the Hill for a meeting.

Senator Ted Poe from Texas.

I'd never been to Capitol Hill and knew very little about the political process. But by the time I was to meet with the congressman, I'd learned everything there was to know.

I was finally going to show up somewhere and say to someone, *I matter.*

The day I walked into the majestic building, I was so nervous. Ma had always taught us kids to show up looking our best. My best was a tailored skirt and jacket, white blouse, boots, and a dark green wool coat with a torn brown belt that I had to staple together because I didn't have the money to buy a new coat.

I met one of my board members at the congressman's office, and then we were quickly ushered through the halls of Congress by his legislative aide to meet the congressman somewhere near the *House Floor*.

"The Congressman will only have a fifteen-minute break in between sessions so you won't have much time. It's best to keep your points short to ensure you get everything in that you want to share with him."

I nodded, trying to keep up with her as we walked, my stapled coat now tucked neatly under my arm, a confident and calm look on my face. Ma would have been so proud of me.

When we reached the *House Floor*, we were hustled into a nearby small conference room. I sat trying to make small talk with the legislative aide all the while rehearsing in my mind what I had studied all week to say.

Once the congressman walked into the room, every ounce of shame about my coat faded. There was a conviction in me that morning despite that I had to staple my broken heart, my home, a man, and my coat.

The congressman was a tall, lean man in his mid-sixties with a pleasant face and sleepy willow eyes. From the moment he opened his mouth with that Southern Texas drawl, I knew he was someone I would come to respect and admire.

"Congressman Poe, I'm so pleased to meet you." I stood, holding out my hand as he warmly embraced it. The moment we took our seats, I lunged into my story and how domestic violence affects millions of women around the globe and why we needed more legislation, prevention, and awareness. Midway through my breathless spiel, the congressman put up his hand and said, "Why do they call you L.Y.? Is that your name?"

I stopped, puzzled. Then told him the story about how since I was a little girl I'd been writing poetry and years later when I decided to embrace my passion and become an author, I wanted to have a cool name so I did some research and came across a story that J.K. Rowling's agent suggested she drop her full name and use only her initials so that the Harry Potter series would have mass appeal.

"It was J.K. Rowling's story that inspired my name, sir."

The congressman looked straight at me with those sleepy willow eyes and said, "That's a very inspiring story but I want to know more about you. Tell me, *who are you?*"

I was at a loss for words.

I knew my life experiences, my aspirations, and my résumé. I had spent the last week preparing to tell him all that there was to know about domestic violence and Saving Promise, but never had I considered *who I was,* nor had anyone ever asked me that question.

I took a deep breath, thought hard about it.

"Sir, I grew up in Wilson Park, one of the most dangerous housing projects in Philadelphia. When I was seventeen years old, I recall sitting on my porch eight months pregnant, in a very abusive relationship, and looking to my left and to my right, and seeing something that would ultimately change my life. I noticed other girls who were about my age and most of us were pregnant, living in poverty and being abused. So I made a decision right then and there that I may be a statistic, but I was *not* going to be a failure.

"Despite growing up in poverty, teen pregnancy, and a terribly abusive relationship, I was the first in my family to go to college. Then as a single mom, I would go on to work for some of the most prestigious corporations in the world, become an award-winning author, and then later walk away from a lucrative corporate career to dedicate my life to Saving Promise. I've invested everything I own to do what I believe in. I lost my mother nearly two years ago, and every day I mourn her; sometimes there are days I don't know how I'm going to get through it. So when I say that I want to help change this global crisis, I truly mean it and I need your help."

The congressman held my eyes. "L.Y., I'm a former judge and prosecutor, and I've seen a lot of domestic violence and how it affects so many people. I think what you are doing is very important, and I like people who stand for what they believe in. So I'm going to do everything I can to help."

That was the first of several meetings with the congressman that led to his personally writing a letter about Saving Promise and sending it to over seventy-five congressmen and congresswomen who were members of the Congressional Victims' Rights Caucus, which he cofounded and cochaired. Later, Congressman Poe invited me to speak at one of the Caucus's forums to share the Saving Promise story. Then he sponsored a congressional briefing for Saving Promise.

To watch the congressional briefing,
visit: lymarlow.com/images

A week prior to the briefing, I walked the halls of Congress, going door to door to more than fifty congressperson's offices telling my story and inviting them to the briefing. By the third door, the words were painted on my heart like calligraphy on a canvas. No longer was I the woman who did not know who she was. I was the woman who got off that floor every day, the woman who wasn't ashamed to go to Congress with staples in her coat and pour out her heart, the woman who believed in her dream.

I was Ma's child, and I *mattered*.

BACON BRA

There are many things that bring me joy, but there is something about shopping for a new bra that just liberates a woman.

In the months following the congressional briefing, I'd spent the time meshing the old with the new—burying myself in my work, writing, and running around the country to speak, not to mention that I was trying to turn over every rock to build Saving Promise, especially those rocks that were tossed my way from Congressman Poe.

Besides, after Tate and I got settled into our apartment, our relationship took on a life of its own. His presence made me feel like I wasn't in this alone. As our lives began to meld together, a sobering thought came over me: if there was to be a future for us, he needed to know *everything*.

On the night that I chose to tell him, I made a special dinner, bought a bottle of wine I couldn't afford, and lit candles. I don't know why I was planning this big romantic production, but somehow pouring my heart out over a candlelit dinner and wine just seemed right to me.

No sooner had Tate gotten home from work and we sat down than I started telling him about how difficult it had been for me to lose Ma, about how I'd walked away from my career and invested everything I owned into Saving Promise, about *Grief* and *Despair*. At some point, I don't know why I threw this in, but I guess it felt good to finally let it all go: I told him that all my bras looked like crispy bacon, and I couldn't even afford to buy a new bra.

There was nothing but silence, sheer silence with Tate's eyes fixed on me.

"First, tomorrow I'm taking you to buy some new bras." Tate smiled, and I felt a smile break through my shame. "And second, you should never be ashamed to talk to me about *anything*. I'm really proud of you, and we're in this together. Okay?"

His eyes were warm and gentle. I liked that he wasn't afraid to express how he felt, that he said he was proud of me, and that he was taking me to get some new bras!

First thing Saturday morning, we went to Target. You would have thought I was a four-year-old in a candy store, helping Tate pick out bras that he thought would look good on me. There is something about shopping for a new bra that just liberates a woman.

It reminded me of a time when I was twelve years old and Ma had taken us girls to Woolworths to buy new bras and panties. I was ecstatic! One, because who didn't love to go to Woolworths? And two, because a new bra meant that I could now hang around the cool girls in my school.

The first day I got to wear my new Fruit of the Loom bra, I stood in front of the mirror looking at how it covered my two button knobs. It didn't matter that the cup size was so small that they could barely hold my finger.

It was *my* bra.

I went to school in it. I slept in it. I did everything in that bra. Wore it like it was a badge of honor.

Over the years, the novelty of my bra wore off. I'd slip it on without ever giving it a second thought. Strange how we trample through our lives taking for granted the things we once treasured. Now, there I stood in the middle of the aisle at Target feeling a sheer sense of humility and gratitude. Holding that bra was like holding a piece of me that had reached back to that twelve-year-old girl who shouted to the world:

I am a woman!

THE UGLY CRY

She never looked nice. She looked like art, and art wasn't supposed to look nice; it was supposed to make you feel something.

—Rainbow Rowell

My new bras armed me with a renewed sense of power. Every morning, I got up and tackled the day like I was tackling a quarterback. I would write from 5:30 a.m. until 10:00 a.m., then turn my attention to Saving Promise, drafting proposals for funding, calling anyone who would listen, accepting any invitation to speak, rationalizing that a new audience opened up new relationships. I'd also decided I was done trying to convince other groups to let me play in their sandbox. It took nearly four years for me to understand the level of competitiveness and territorialism that persisted in the domestic violence community, which I found laughable because we were all supposedly striving toward the same goal: *to help people.* But my laughter came with the realization that if I was serious about making a difference, then I had to go at it alone.

But *alone* didn't mean that I had to do it all by myself. It meant that I had to fall back on my roots: *the hard knocks of growing up in Wilson Park and my corporate upbringing.*

First, I developed a savvy business strategy to brand Saving Promise with a new mission focused on prevention, then I engaged a public relations firm who took on Saving Promise pro bono. The day I met with the public relations firm, I sat across the table from Ann, the managing director, surrounded by her team of public affairs and communications experts and poured my heart out. By now, after my encounter with the purple cross, I wasn't afraid to wear my heart on my sleeve. Hell, I had nothing to lose, and I'd since given up any notion that it was a sign of weakness to be vulnerable. In fact, the only thing I had going for myself was vulnerability. So when I sat across from Ann and her team, I spoke with conviction. The same conviction that I woke up with every morning, ready to bulldoze my way to a better place. Meanwhile, my extenuating circumstances had another plan. What little savings I had was quickly running out, the doors I was knocking on for funding went unanswered, and when I showed up at different places to speak, I was met with empty promises. If I didn't raise funds soon, it would be the end for Saving Promise and me.

With no firm leads, I went to my bank where I had been banking for more than fifteen years and met with the branch manager. Tall and stout with a pleasant clean-shaven face, Ed Sanders had come to know me from the frequent visits that I made to the branch, and he enthusiastically ushered me into his office. Although Ed saw me at least once a week, he knew little about Saving Promise except that it was a nonprofit that I was running and probably not so well from the looks of our accounts.

The moment I sat down with Ed, I started telling him the Saving Promise story and my new plan, and then I got real honest. "I've been banking here since I first moved to the area, and I know you give back to the community. I'm hoping that you'll consider Saving Promise for a grant. We could really use the funds."

Ed looked at me with compassion. "Your story and mission are very inspiring, and I'd be happy to submit your organization to our corporate giving program. Why don't you send me some materials and let me see what I can do?"

I went home and wrote a proposal and sent it to Ed by email and also hand delivered a copy to him the next morning to ensure he received it.

Over the next several weeks, I called friends, family, and acquaintances—anyone who would listen. Meanwhile, Ann arranged a brainstorming session with her team to revitalize the Saving Promise brand and help us build new relationships.

"It's going to take some time, L.Y.," Ann had said to me on a call one day. "But we can get some quick wins and start moving toward the new vision."

While I knew the public relations firm had potential for Saving Promise, there was no silver bullet; it could take years to build the brand. But I also knew I needed to figure out how to cut down the time.

Later, when I received an email from Ed asking me to come to the branch to meet with him, I felt optimistic. Surely we had been approved for the grant. The questions were how much and would it be enough to sustain us?

I arrived at the bank the next morning as soon as they opened and was pleasantly surprised to see Ed already there. Again, he ushered me into his office, and I anxiously took the seat across from him.

"I asked you in because I wanted to give you the news in person and not over email or the phone." He looked at me this time with no smile on his face. "I'm really sorry to inform you that the bank denied your grant request."

"*What?*"

"I tried. I even called to see why they denied it. Part of the problem is that they only give to certain types of organizations, and Saving Promise does not meet that criteria."

"But I've been banking here for more than fifteen years and Saving Promise's accounts are here and I've been a good customer and we have a good mission and we are trying to help people and I'm running out of funds and why can't you help me?!"

The next thing I knew, I was panting and the tears started flowing and my face started twitching, and there I was, this hysterical black woman with the ugly cry and this middle-aged white man who looked like he was ready to bolt.

And I didn't blame him. I would have gotten the hell out of there too.

Instead, Ed came around his desk, closed the door, and took the seat next to me.

"My wife and I wanted to give you this." He handed me an envelope with a personal check inside. "It's not much, but I think what you are doing is good work. I know things are tough, but it will all work out and maybe we can try again next year with the bank."

I pulled myself together before I left Ed's office, went home, and slept for hours. I was exhausted. I'd also noticed the strange heart palpitations and shortness of breath I'd been getting lately made their presence known. The next day I made an emergency appointment to see my doctor and told him about my symptoms. He took copious notes, asked a lot of questions, and gave me a full physical and blood workup.

Hours later, when he walked back into the exam room, he said, "All your labs came back okay. The EKG shows no sign of heart trouble, but you are having anxiety attacks, and we can treat it one of two ways: with medication or therapy."

"Anxiety attacks? I'm not having any anxiety attacks!"

"Yes! You are having anxiety attacks. With everything that's going on in your life, you are under tremendous stress, which can trigger these attacks."

"Well I don't need to see no therapist or take medication because mental illness runs in my family and I know I'm not mentally ill."

"You don't have to take the medication, but I would recommend cognitive behavioral therapy, which is very effective for treating anxiety; it will also help you manage your stress."

After having to live with the memory of my sister Angie's dismembered body, which I had to identify after she jumped in front of a train (a memory I profoundly carried for many, many years to spare Ma from having to see the body of her youngest child), I'd spent most of my life trying to avoid ever being remotely labeled with anything that looked, felt, or smelled like mental illness.

My mind went back to the look on Ma's face when she learned that Angie had been diagnosed with a manic-depressive disorder and schizophrenia; back to the "episodes" (that's what they called the voices Angie heard, the things she imagined); back to the countless psychiatrists, treatment centers, and hospitals that Ma took her to; back to the first of many times she tried to commit suicide; back to the day that I'd gotten the call a few days shy of her nineteenth birthday; back to her face, her dismembered body.

Angie was part of a long line of mental illness that ran in my family. And while *Grief* and *Despair* still loomed and I'd go as far to say that I was even a little depressed, I was *not* mentally ill. I sat there feeling the palpitations in my chest. I didn't want to lie on anybody's couch reflecting back on my childhood.

"Look, I know you're concerned about trying therapy, but I can refer you to someone who specializes in cognitive behavioral therapy. I really recommend you make an appointment to see her, and if you don't feel comfortable after that first session, then we can come up with another plan. How does that sound?"

"Alright. I'll go," I finally said, barely a whisper.

"Good, I'll print out the referral, which will have all of her information, and let's plan to have you come back for a visit with me if you don't find her helpful."

Two weeks later I showed up on Dr. Vicki Mercer's *couch*.

Dr. Vicki—who I asked if it was okay to call her this instead of Dr. Mercer because I wanted it to feel more like I was talking to one of my girlfriends instead of a psychologist—had a friendly personality and a face framed by soft blond hair.

There was something about Dr. Vicki that I immediately liked and made me open up my mind and my mouth. Before I knew it, I told her *everything*. Things I had never even told myself.

The whole time, Dr. Vicki took notes and just let me talk and talk and talk. By the time our first session was over, I was exhausted and I know I exhausted her too.

"We've got some work to do, don't we?"

I nodded, embarrassed.

Every week, there I was on Dr. Vicki's *couch*, emptying my head and my heart. I talked about my relationships with men, my work, Ma, my finances, my family, my stress. At some point, Dr. Vicki recommended meditation. *It will help center you.*

I had tried meditating in the past, but it never really stuck because I couldn't get my mind to shut up long enough to give me a moment of silence. Then one evening I watched *America's Most Unusual Town* on OWN (the Oprah Winfrey Network) where Oprah visited a town in Fairfield, Iowa, that had very little mess, mayhem, or stress because nearly the whole town meditated. After learning about Transcendental Meditation, I discovered that there was a TM center thirty-five minutes from where I lived. I called and got invited to attend an orientation the following Saturday.

I went not expecting much. But the moment I met Linda and her husband, Mario, who ran the TM center in Rockville, Maryland, their generous and loving spirit broke me into pieces. There I was with the ugly cry again, pleading for help.

"I was having anxiety attacks because of all the stress with Saving Promise and my work, and I miss my mother, and I don't hardly have any money left to live, and I'm in a relationship but I don't want to burden him with my problems, and I can't afford to pay for the TM program, and Dr. Vicki suggested that I try meditation . . . and . . . and . . . and . . ."

Linda reached out and took me in her arms. "Don't you worry. TM will help with the stress and everything you're dealing with, and the TM center has a grant program."

I was a broken mess. But for the first time in a long time, I felt like I was going to be okay. *Maybe*, I thought, as I sank deeper into Linda's arms and let her hold me.

FROM BAD . . .

Ma always said things can go from bad to worse before they get better.

My bad started soon after I learned to meditate. Within a few weeks, it was like plunging downhill with no brakes. First, John was diagnosed with a heart condition. Then I received a certified letter from the IRS threatening to take all of my assets, which was followed by American Express threatening to sue me because I could no longer afford the exorbitant payments on the business account I had used to pay the bills for Saving Promise. But nothing was worse than attending the funeral of my sister's youngest son, who broke his neck in a freak accident.

I sat in the church, blank-faced, and watched Eileen trying to be brave. Outside, the sun poured down on the countless cars that lined the streets and the infinite number of young people waiting to come inside.

I had never thought about death. Even when Ma had died, it didn't feel like death to me. It felt more like Ma was passing from one life to another. But seeing Eileen and all those young people grieving over a casket that held the remains of my nephew, I wanted to scream: *Death.*

There we were again—Ma's kids—staring at a casket, swollen with grief. I sat next to Eileen with a bottomless pit of tears, trying to find comfort in my own words. *He's with Ma.* That's what I'd told her the day I got the news and then did what I had always done—tried to *fix* it. I helped raise funds for the funeral, gathered the family, and tried to manage Eileen's grief. I didn't know what else to do or to say when I saw the same anguish on Eileen's face that I had seen on Ma's when Angie had died. There are no words, no wisdom that can comfort a mother who has lost her child.

That evening, I drove back home. I wanted to stay, but I just couldn't face death. *Death* made me think about all the people in my family who had died—Mama, Ma, my father, my sister, and my nephew. *Death* reminded me of all the moments I wasted being angry, resentful, unforgiving; taught me how to practice spirituality; forced me into humility; and chastised me when I didn't show gratitude. *Death* scared me. Partly because I felt like a part of me had died and partly because I was still struggling to live.

When I got home, I lay on the sofa in my pajamas and dreamed of my grandmother Mama. *Your time has come.* That's all she kept saying to me over and over again. *Your time has come.*

"No, please don't take me. I'm not ready yet," I'd begged just before I jumped from my sleep. I lay awake all night, afraid to close my eyes.

That dream had shaken me so much that I wrote a poem about it.

My eyes were closed, though I could see
What clearly lay ahead of me

A bright light shone, before my eyes
The voice I heard, spoke no compromise

Your time has come, it simply said
to take the tour, towards heavens stairs

I cannot go, justly I proclaimed
this hallowed life, I must sustain

There is no escape, for what's set and done
You've been chosen, your time has come

Free me please, for I cannot bear
What fate has paved, for this guided tour
My life is meek, compared to thee
But my heart will bleed for my family

Though I somehow know, the exult of heaven's ways
I beg your pardon—extend my earthly days

The light withdrew, as she closed the door
On my final fate, for heaven's tour

I shall move on, though I hope and pray
that heaven's tour, will come my way again someday.

The Tour

That's what I felt like as I lay on that sofa, like I was on a tour and *Death* was all around me. In the walls, the rug, the kitchen, on the sofa beside me. Never before had I thought so much about *Death,* but there is something about a young person dying that makes you think about living.

The next morning, I called to check on John. Since Ma had passed, John's health had declined, and I'd been going back and forth to Lugoff to spend time with him, clean the house, and cook and freeze enough food that would last until I returned again.

He'd been diagnosed with a heart murmur, and the doctors decided to monitor it instead of doing open-heart surgery because they said he would have a fifty-fifty chance of survival.

I'd read about how the grief of losing a spouse can affect the health of the surviving spouse, oftentimes leading to their loss.

Watching John after losing Ma was like watching a baby cub that had been separated from its mother. He didn't know how to live without her. Every day he'd go through the same motions: eat oatmeal, a bagel, and and banana for breakfast; a turkey sandwich or salad for lunch; and beans or whatever I'd cooked months prior and left in the freezer for dinner. Then he'd go back to their bedroom where he spent all of his time sitting in his La-Z-Boy watching TV, listening to the radio, or learning to play the keyboard—a hobby he took up a few years after Ma passed. But let me tell you, if I had to hear him play "Mary had a Little Lamb" or "Blueberry Hill" or any of the limited number of songs he liked to dab away at on his keyboard one more time, I was going to scream! Other than that, he'd go to the doctors or Walmart, and on Sundays, he'd go to church as a penance to Ma.

Now, I felt a rush of sad emotion when I finally heard John's voice on the other end of the line.

"How was the funeral? How's Eileen doing? I probably should have gone."

He had not attended the funeral because the doctor thought it probably wasn't a good idea for him to travel. I agreed because this would have been the first funeral he would have attended since losing Ma; a part of me was relieved he hadn't been there.

"No. It was a good thing that you didn't go. Eileen was fine. The family's going to be just fine. We're all going to get through this."

As I imagined John sitting there in his La-Z-Boy, I couldn't help but think about the irony of his broken heart.

Over the next few months, I dreaded the calls and the letters I'd written to the IRS and American Express. In every communication, every conversation, I was utterly and profoundly pleading for *my dignity.*

Years earlier, I'd inherited a tax debt after filing a joint tax return with my first husband, which resulted in the IRS seizing my bank accounts and confiscating my paychecks for back taxes that my ex owed.

This time when I received the letter from the IRS threatening to confiscate all of my assets after my accountant failed to file my tax return electronically, the thought of dealing with the IRS again was like diving off a cliff and hoping to land on supple ground. Then there was American Express threatening to take action against me too.

And assets? What assets?

I prayed. I meditated. I talked to Dr. Vicki about it. I wrote letters and called, pleading with the IRS and American Express. I felt like a giant beast was standing on my chest. I didn't want to go to my family; I didn't want to bother John.

I didn't know what else to do, and I had nowhere else to turn. I cringed at the idea of turning to the only person I thought could help me.

Tate.

TO WORSE

There are three things I have come to learn as my biggest lessons:

1. *Worse isn't always so bad, especially when its purpose is to make you better.*
2. *Always ask, what is this experience here to teach me?*
3. *Trust in God and the universe.*

I don't remember the exact words I used when I confessed to Tate. All I remember was the fear of having to face the IRS and American Express and what would happen to me if they took what little money I had.

I had tried so hard to keep my problems from Tate that it never occurred to me that he would want to help. First, Tate offered to cover the bulk of our daily expenses so that I could work out something with the IRS. Then he agreed to make the minimum monthly payments that I owed to American Express to keep them from filing the suit against me.

I promised Tate that I would pay him back every cent, and for the first time since we'd been together, I felt like I didn't have to be ashamed anymore.

Shortly after my talk with Tate, things were finally looking up. To begin with, Saving Promise received its first grant from The Unity Fund for Sustained Change, a component fund of the Community Foundation for the National Capital Region in Washington DC. I'd met one of their board members the year prior who had heard me speak at a fundraising event that a mutual friend held at his home. He'd come up to me afterward and told me that he was moved by my story and wanted to help. That conversation led to our first grant for $25K. I was so elated, you would have thought I was holding a check for a million bucks.

UFFSC First Grant, October 2012, Washington, DC
To view, visit: lymarlow.com/images

While that check had lifted my spirit, I also knew that if we didn't raise more funds, Saving Promise wouldn't survive. So shortly after, I scheduled a meeting with the board and got real honest with myself. It was time we rolled up our sleeves.

As the board meeting loomed, I drafted a plan and met with a few of the board members to solicit their input. Rather than focus on the past, I viewed this as a seminal moment with immense opportunity to reposition Saving Promise. I was a bit nervous about the meeting because I knew that if it was a struggle for me to get honest with myself, then it would be a struggle for the board.

On the day of the board meeting, something just didn't feel right. I knew that either the meeting was going to be a huge success or a complete failure. Despite the outcome, I'd decided that I would still move forward. I owed that much to myself, my family, Promise, and the millions of women and children who suffered daily from domestic violence. Moreover, I'd come to realize that no one would ever be as passionate about Saving Promise as I, and I shouldn't expect that they would have the same dedication or vision. They had not made the sacrifices I had made. That purple cross did not speak to them the way it had spoken to me. Nor had they heard a three-year-old little girl's words of wisdom.

I knew I was about to take a risk, but it was a risk worth taking.

The moment the board took their seats, I could feel the tension in the room, a strain lurking over me. I looked around the table at the five women and one man and listened intently to the silence from the other two on the phone, one male and one female. I knew the plan they were brewing wasn't the plan I was proposing. I'd also called a few of the same board members I had spoken to prior to the meeting, and when they didn't return my call, I knew something was up.

I opened the meeting by outlining the agenda, and then I moved right into my proposal. I reminded them of the discussions we'd had with the public relations firm to rebrand Saving Promise, the critical state of the organization, and the need to raise funds. I also reminded them about how overburdened I was and recommended that we use the new grant to secure a consultant to help us raise enough funds to hire a COO and development director to stabilize the organization, and then appealed to them for help.

I was surprised when one of the board members spoke up. "We've been giving thought to how best to manage Saving Promise and given how overburdened you are, we recommend that one of the other board members oversee the day-to-day operations and fundraising efforts to generate operating income so that your time would be freed to focus on building relationships and the brand."

First, I had called this board member earlier that day, and she never called me back. Second, the board member who they were recommending to run the daily operations and raise funds was one of the few who *had* returned my call that day and said she was very concerned about what they were proposing. During the conversation, she confided in me that not only did she not have the time to commit, but also she didn't know the first thing about running a nonprofit. I agreed, at her request, to hold our discussion in confidence. When the recommendation was suggested at the meeting, I waited for her to speak up and when she did not, I did.

"This would require a full-time commitment that I'm not convinced this board member is able to commit, and more importantly, raising funds should be the collective fiscal responsibility of the entire board, including me, and not be left to one board member. Therefore, I ask that you reconsider my request to hire a consultant to help us raise the funds that can be used to bring on a COO and development director."

There was a tenuous cynicism in the air as a few of the board members started to speak up, either agreeing with my recommendations, resisting, or being neutral. Then one board member began to talk, and from the way she spoke, I could tell that she was the ringleader, even making a few sarcastic remarks at my expense.

Quite frankly, I was taken aback by the *ringleader* because she was the one person I trusted the most, the one I'd turned to for guidance, confided in, and took to all the important meetings, including the meeting with Congressman Poe.

For the next hour, I listened to the board's assertions and fielded questions, then wrapped up the meeting with the board agreeing unanimously to appoint the lone board member (who had spoken to me confidence but still said nothing about her concerns) to oversee the operations and fundraising.

I drove home feeling more discouraged and depleted than ever. I had never liked confrontations, especially those with a hidden agenda. While I wasn't sure how things would turn out, there was one thing that was absolutely clear to me: either they were going to help or they were not. But I was *not* going to allow Saving Promise to fail because of someone's ego or bureaucracy.

I would stand up for what I believed in.

Over the next few days, I reached out to the board member they'd appointed to offer to help with the operations and fund-raising. When she finally agreed to a call after a week of trying to pin down a time in her schedule, I wasn't surprised when she told me that she had accepted a new position and didn't have the time to commit. I encouraged her to inform the board so that we could come up with another plan.

Meanwhile, I'd been invited to appear on MSNBC's *Melissa Harris-Perry Show* to participate in a panel discussion on the Violence Against Women Act (VAWA). I spoke with conviction because I guess I was still reeling from the way I was being treated by the board. Besides, no one had volunteered to step up to help after they learned that the lone board member could not make the commitment. My instinct was to take control of the situation, but ego-playing was not an option for me. I was not about to waste what little time and energy I had left to consort with their tactics. Nor was I going to put Saving Promise at further risk by doing something that could hurt the organization. So when the *ringleader* sent an email and copied all the board members, clearly intending to pick a fight, I simply chose to ignore it. I was not about to join her in a schoolyard brawl or allow her to bully me. Instead, I emailed her separately, asking for just the two of us to meet—an email that went unanswered.

To view and read the blog, visit: lymarlow.com/images

A few days later, I was stunned to receive a letter of resignation from the board citing that I was resistant to their recommendations. All but two had signed the letter. Without a board, Saving Promise could lose its 501(c)(3) status.

I had not seen it coming.

To say that I was distraught is an understatement. I simply went to bed. When Tate returned home, he found me with the blinds drawn and the blanket over my head.

"You can't let them take away your dream. You've come too far. You have to be stronger. And don't you dare respond to that letter. Ignore it for now."

I tried desperately to listen to Tate, but I'd had enough! I was tired of floundering. I was tired of fighting. I was just plain tired.

The next day, the two board members—the ones who had not signed the letter—reached out to me. I waited a few days until I pulled myself together before I met with them. By then, my agony had turned to anger, but not the bad anger. It was the kind that hauled my ass out of that bed and told me I had to fight—if not for myself, for Ma.

When I met with the two board members, I didn't mince words, nor did I try to scapegoat anyone, including myself, for the board's resignation. I simply stated the facts—that at no time was I ever resistant to any of the board's recommendations—and followed it up with a letter of explanation that outlined a response to the reasons that the board had used to resign.

> *"After much reflection and counsel, I was advised that in order to reinstate your trust in my integrity and leadership, and more importantly, preserve the integrity and credibility of the organization, it would be best to document the facts that led up to the resignation of the board on March 11, 2013. . . . While I regret the loss of any board member, I am committed as ever to stay the course and lead the organization towards our shared vision."*

After reviewing all the materials, they both expressed their outrage for the way that the board had tried to stage a coup to undermine the organization. "We are going to stick by you, L.Y.," they promised. It was a relief, because I'd learned that the IRS requires that at least three distinct individuals must serve on the board in order to retain a 501(c)(3) nonexempt status. Since I had never taken a salary from the organization and technically also served as a volunteer, I could be counted as a board member along with the other two. I'd also learned that the board members' actions were not only unethical, but they could be held personally liable for gross negligence.

I'd decided that either I could focus my time and energy on trying to hold them accountable or on building Saving Promise.

I did some soul searching and thought back on a Joel Osteen sermon entitled *A Shift Is Coming* that I'd watched one Sunday morning when things were heating up with the board. "With one touch from God things could shift in your favor. You could be going along being your best, honoring God, and suddenly things change. One good break. One idea. One person that likes you . . . you didn't see it coming. Things just fell into place," he preached. "That's God shifting things in your favor . . . What used to be a struggle, is not a struggle anymore . . . You may feel like you're stuck today. Like you'll never accomplish your dream, never overcome a problem . . . but that's God saying: *Get ready, I'm about to shift things.*"

I chose Saving Promise.

I wasn't sure how, what, or when one good idea, one good break, or one good person would come. The only thing I knew for sure was that I needed to pray and ask God for . . . *a shift*.

THE SHIFT

If The Shift meant that I was about to lose everything, including me, then I'm not sure I was ready for what God had in mind.

Shortly after the board resigned, I stood in the lobby of my apartment complex holding a summons that had been handed to me by a stranger who said, without the least bit of expression on his face, *You've been served.*

American Express was suing me!

The minimum payments that Tate was making on my behalf apparently weren't good enough. And if that wasn't bad enough, I'd also just found out that I was a victim of identity theft that targeted what little credit and savings I had left. It forced me to shut down all of my accounts and spend months trying to recover.

Not only was I robbing Peter to pay Paul, but I had robbed my life savings, liquidated my retirement accounts, walked away from a prosperous career, borrowed money from friends and family, been audited by the IRS, sued by American Express, became a victim of identity theft, and taken on considerable debt all in the name of *Purpose.*

It was once exciting to discover *Purpose.* In fact, I wouldn't even say that I discovered her. It was more like she snatched me up from the time I was eight years old. Always the thoughtful, ambitious, strange child, I knew my life was meant for something bigger. When my siblings were out *ripping and running,* as Ma called it, I was barricaded in my room organizing my Barbies or crafting my life plan or reading poetry from Edgar Allen Poe, a heritage to my grade school with the same name. It came as no coincidence that by the age of seventeen, as I sat on my porch in

Wilson Park Projects after being viciously beaten and kicked in my eight-months-pregnant belly by my boyfriend, I would make a promise to myself that this was not to be my life.

I'd once watched a segment on Oprah's *Lifeclass* entitled *Living with Purpose* where Oprah and Bishop T.D. Jakes talked about how you may start out doing one thing that leads you to the *thing* that you were created to do, and that you shouldn't look at your experiences as the destination but rather as the transportation that brings you into your purpose.

Lightbulb moment: *I got it!*

But still I struggled with the notion that reading a stanza from Edgar Allen Poe or being kicked in my eight-months-pregnant belly or going to school for sixteen years at night only to walk away from a lucrative career and be stripped of everything I owned was leading me to my destiny.

But *Purpose* told me that if I walked away from fate I would never be forgiven; that my life was not my own.

Now, after being handed the summons, I went back to my apartment and called Tate at work. I didn't know who else to call. I was tired of calling on God because it seemed like the more I prayed, the more I was being *served*.

"You need to hire an attorney," was all I got from Tate.

The next morning I found a bankruptcy attorney and showed up at his office with an armful of bills, begging for help.

He took notes, asked a lot of questions, and then meticulously scanned through my files.

"So here's the thing." He finally looked straight at me. "American Express has filed suit against you *and* you are in financial ruin, so you have no choice but to file bankruptcy. My fee is fifteen hundred dollars plus court fees, which are about an additional three hundred dollars notwithstanding any unforeseeable fees that may arise, so the whole process will cost you anywhere between eighteen hundred and two thousand dollars. I need half of my fee and the court fees as a retainer before I can take you on as my client."

"I don't have that kind of money! Is there any way you can work with me, maybe a payment plan or something?"

He looked at me with what appeared to be annoyance.

"First, the law doesn't allow you to retain me on a payment plan because then I become one of your creditors that need to be named in the bankruptcy. Second, and I don't mean to be rude, but from the looks of your circumstances, you can't afford a payment plan. Do you have family or a friend who can lend you the money?"

I started to cry. I didn't intend to cry, but I'd done it so much by now that crying had become a natural reaction.

They say lawyers don't have a soul, but if you want to scare the baby Jesus out of a man, lawyer or not, just start crying.

So there I was with my ugly cry again, a wreck.

"Ms. Marlow, maybe I'll take a closer look at your file and if you're able to come up with half of my fees and be willing to help with preparing all the documentation, I may take on your case. Would that work for you?"

I took the tissue he handed to me and blew my nose. "I can talk to my family and see what I can come up with."

"Alright then. Why don't you do that and give me a call in a few days."

When I got home, I told Tate about my meeting with the attorney. I'd noticed over the past year since we had the first talk about my finances and *Grief, Despair, and Purpose,* he had started to retreat and reveal another side of him. The Tate who was caring and comforting had become less attentive and more resentful and insecure. Then came the heated arguments that often led to his accusing me of using him and seeing other men, which wasn't the least bit true. I was in no condition to be man-chasing. I barely had enough time and energy to invest in our relationship. Besides which, I began to realize that it had nothing to do with other men, and more to do with the fact that I had become too much and too needy, and the more I latched on to him, the more he withdrew.

This went on for months until one day I found myself sitting alone in a park under a tree with bird droppings falling on me. The intensity and bitter anger that Tate lashed out at me this time ripped my already delicate heart to pieces. I came to fear that he would eventually leave, which sent me clinging to *Lonely*.

It's your fault if he leaves. You and Purpose always pushing people away!

Lonely was brutal this time as I sat there under that tree in tears, not caring that I had bird droppings in my hair, on my arms and legs, on my clothes. I deserved it!

When I finally returned home six hours later covered in bird shit, I wasn't surprised to see that Tate had packed his bags.

"I didn't sign up for all of this. I'm leaving!"

Now, you would have thought that sitting in the park for six hours would have prepared me to accept that it was over. But instead, I allowed *Lonely* to push me into a deeper state of panic.

"Please, don't leave! I can change! We can change! I'll get a job. Please!"

Tate ignored me as he packed his clothes, his things, anything of value, except me. I was no more valuable to him than the sofa and bedroom furnishings he left behind.

Over the next few weeks, I went through the motions like a zombie: I'd get up, meditate, stumble through my day, go back to bed, and cry myself to sleep. I'd get up, meditate, stumble through my day, go back to bed, and cry myself to sleep. Soon, I went to see Dr. Vicki and when she escorted me into her office, I slumped down on the *couch* and cried.

Just cried.

"It will get better. It always gets better," Dr. Vicki encouraged.

But I couldn't see *better*. All I could see was the sheer anguish over how I was going to pay my bills or where I would live or how I was going to even buy groceries.

By the time I emptied myself out on Dr. Vicki's *couch* and returned home, I called John and asked him for help.

John agreed to lend me enough money to pay my bills for six months and hire a bankruptcy attorney. Shortly after, I moved into a smaller apartment and hired a more affordable bankruptcy attorney.

Weeks later, as I sat in bankruptcy court waiting to go before the judge, I received a disturbing email. It said: *L. Y. Your story has run its course . . .* Though those callous words cut through me like a knife, I won't dignify the rest of what it said in this book.

There I was sitting in bankruptcy court because I'd given everything I owned to Saving Promise, including me, and someone had the nerve to be so cruel. I will never understand how people could be so vicious, especially when you've done nothing but been kind and decent. Early on, when I first started Saving Promise, I would beg people to stay, figuratively clutching to their ankles, dragging me to the door. I was still very fragile and often questioning if I'd made the right decision to give up my corporate career. When people came along to help, I clung to them for fear of doing it on my own. But after endless bruised elbows and knees from all the begging and dragging, I found comfort and courage in something I once heard someone say: *When people are ready to leave you, let them.* That clicked for me.

Soon, I had come to accept that everyone who came along on my journey was there to serve a purpose and when that purpose was done, whatever it was—whether to teach me something, to shepherd me along, or merely just to take up space—*let them go.*

So that's what I'd did. I got real still and let them go with grace. Interestingly enough, what that has taught me is that for the ones who leave in peace leave with gratitude. But those who leave in peril didn't take kindly to gratitude or grace. They wanted to see me suffer and when I didn't (at least I never showed them *Suffering*), they'd undoubtedly always came back to twist the knife.

This woman was one of those *twisters.* One of the women who had quit a few years before with the other women that had all gotten together to submit their resignation at the same time Ma was dying. Because my heart was already broken, I didn't have any more hurt to give. Besides which, I was far along in my *let-them-go* centeredness that when they had tried to hurt me, I had sent them all a kind email wishing them well.

But by now after years of deflecting the daggers, when the judge called my name, I was so emotionally, physically, spiritually, and financially *Bankrupt* that I just stood there answering his questions with little more than a whisper. Then I went home, crawled back in bed, and slept.

At 4:30 a.m. I was shaken from my sleep to a strange noise. I knew it was 4:30 a.m. because I looked over at the clock, and when I turned to lie back down, I heard my bedroom door open, and there was Ma walking toward me. She looked so pretty, peace on her face.

You're not supposed to be here. You were sick and then you left us, I cried. I couldn't say died because still I was afraid of *Death,* and *Death* wasn't at my door; Ma was. Before I could say anything more, she got in the bed, put her arms around me, and rocked me back to sleep.

The next morning I jumped up, my heart pounding my chest. *She was here . . . Ma was here . . . she was real . . .* I kept saying to myself, hysterical, then rushed into the living room as if I would find Ma sitting on the sofa.

Part of me wanted it to be real, and another part of me was terrified.

I'd recalled the time Ma had told me that my daddy had visited her the night that he'd died. I sat across from her taking notes for *Color Me Butterfly* as she told me the story:

Roy lay in the hospital in a coma for more than a week the night I'd put ya'll to bed, taken my bath and had gotten into bed; and when I turned off the lights, there he was, the same two surgical patches that covered his eyes, she said, her face drawn into the memory. *I watched him as he removed the patches and looked at me, just looked at me, and then he was gone. The next day the police showed up at my door and told me he had passed.*

I'd never forgotten that story, and as certain as Ma had been when she'd said Daddy was real—that's how *real* Ma had been to me at that moment.

Over the next several weeks, I somehow made it through the day, but at night I was reduced to crying spells, consumed by *Grief, Despair, Purpose, Bankrupt*. It had gotten so bad that I'd just kneel on the floor begging for mercy.

I couldn't eat. I couldn't sleep. I couldn't *live*.

Finally, I called my girlfriend Erica whom I'd met at the TM center and the moment she heard my voice, she said, "I want to put you in touch with a spiritual teacher."

I sobbed into the phone, "But I don't have any money to pay her."

"Don't you worry about that. I'm going to ask her if she'll waive her fee, and if not, I'll pay for it."

Two days later I sat with the phone pressed against my ear listening to Beatriz, a spiritual teacher from San Antonio, Texas; her soothing voice immediately brought light into my heart and home.

"Tell me about you."

"About me?" I stammered. Quite frankly, I wasn't sure *who* *I* was anymore. So I started to tell her about Saving Promise and my work.

"No," she interrupted. "Tell me who *you* are. Where did you grow up? Tell me about your family."

For some reason, my mind shifted back to my father's funeral when I was five years old, standing on my tiptoes, my small hands grasping at the edges of his casket, trying to get a glimpse of him inside. That memory is as painted in my mind as color is to a canvas.

I sobbed as I told her about my childhood and growing up in Wilson Park; about my family and our history with domestic violence; about being a single mom and going to school at night and walking away from my career; about Saving Promise, the challenges, and all the people who had come and gone; and about my relationships with men, and Tate, the hurt and pain it all had caused me.

Over the next few days, Beatriz meticulously uprooted every aspect of my life as though she were performing a delicate open heart surgery. And, in a way, she was beginning to open my heart and mind as it had never been opened before.

At one point when I told her about Tate, her voice became very honest: "Tate could never be the man you deserve and need. He did you a favor by leaving."

Then she spoke emphatically about how we all are infinite spiritual beings made in the image of God and every one of us has a true nature. But to tap into our true nature, we must be willing to move beyond the illusions of the world. We must begin embracing our life experiences, our hardships, as lessons.

"What and who we attract into our lives are intended to serve a higher purpose. The pain that Tate and others have caused you was a gift. You must begin to see this pain as an opportunity for spiritual growth.

"But in order to grow, you must first forgive. I have an exercise called *The Miracle of Self-Healing* that will help you to forgive and heal. I want you to go to my website and find this exercise and I want you to walk through the eight steps that I have outlined. There's also a guided meditation and other materials that will help you though this process.

"Now, there is something I want to say to you and you need to hear me."

I closed my eyes and got *real* still.

"You have been put on this earth for a purpose. Saving Promise *is* your purpose and you are going to do extraordinary things that will change so many lives. But until you surrender and come to understand that life is happening *for you* and not *to you*, you will never be able to able to reach your higher purpose. As long as you continue to resist your true nature, your life will remain the same. You must *surrender*. Do you understand?"

I didn't know how to surrender and how all this bad stuff was happening *for me*. I wiped the tears from my face and closed my eyes against the dim candlelit room.

"Yes, I understand," I finally said, still unsure.

Over the next few days, I spent hours on Beatriz's website, meditated, started a gratitude journal, and prayed.

Life is happening for me, not to me, I chanted day after day. *Life is happening for me, not to me. Life is happening for me, not to me.*

A few weeks later, I went to spend Christmas Eve with my daughter and Promise. I'd wrapped small gifts that I had bought with the money I'd put aside for my groceries and a used Raggedy Ann doll that Geraldine—a French woman who had recently joined Saving Promise—had given me for Promise from a stash of old toys her teenage daughter no longer needed. I knew she'd given me that doll because she suspected I couldn't afford to buy a doll for Promise.

When I arrived, I could tell something just wasn't right with Treasure. I'd seen that look many times before since she had been dating a man who I'd met briefly when she invited him to dinner a few months prior. One look at him, and I could tell he was no good.

"Are you okay?" I watched her face in the dimly lit small living room that was decked in Christmas decor. The tree, the room, everything seemed festive but her.

"I'm fine, Mom."

I tried to hold her eyes, but she turned away.

"No, you're not fine. I could see it on your face. Please talk to me."

"Mom, let's not spoil Christmas. I'm fine, okay."

I looked at the sadness on her face, the brokenness. "You're not fine. Please talk to me. I promise not to spoil Christmas, and I won't judge you. Please!"

She finally held my eyes, then slowly unwrapped the sweater around her small frame and pulled her hair back away from her face and neck.

I gasped.

There were hand marks around her neck, bruises on her arms and legs, a bite mark on her back, and now I could see the swelling on her face and that she had lost so much weight.

"Bobby did this to me, Mom. But we've talked about it, and he's not going to do it again. We're fine now."

"My God! Not again, Treasure! You got to get out of this right now! Please!"

"See, Mom, you promised not to do this. You promised!"

"But look at you! Look at you!"

"Mom, please don't do this! Please don't spoil Christmas! I'm fine. Bobby and I are fine! He's coming to Christmas dinner with us and you have to promise not to say anything to him. Please, Mom!"

"What?! I'm not sitting across the table sharing Christmas dinner with that man! I will *not*!"

"Please! Maybe you can talk to him. He wants to change!"

I looked her straight in the eyes. "The only thing I will do if he shows up here is call the police!"

"See, you said you wouldn't do this. You promised!"

There are moments in your life when you told yourself you never wanted to look or sound like your own mother (at least some parts of her). That night, I heard Ma's voice rise through me like lightning.

"I'm sorry if I broke my promise to you! But I'm your mother, and you can't expect me to do nothing. Now, I'll say it again. If he shows up here, I'm calling the police!"

"Alright, Mom! I won't have him come to dinner. But he's living with me now so he will be here at some point, and you're going to have to respect my decision."

"You're right! I may have to respect your decision, but I don't have to be a part of it. I'll spend Christmas Eve with you and Promise, but I'm leaving in the morning."

"You don't have to leave, Mom. I'll make sure he's not here when you're here."

I gave her Ma's *look* again. "Why, Treasure? You deserve better! You don't need him!"

"Mom, stop! You have to let me live my life and make my own choices!"

Every fiber in my body wanted to take her in my arms and protect her from her own sense of selflessness, to remind her of all the pain Mama, Ma, me, and she had been through—and Promise. What about *Promise*?

But she was just too lost in the tunnel of darkness with no light to find her way out.

She was broken. I was broken. We were broken. And there was nothing more I could say; nothing more I could do but . . . *surrender.*

PART 3

THE BLESSINGS

"Surrender to what is. Let go of what was.
Have faith in what will be."
–Sonia Ricott

It's Horrifying

Surrendering can be downright horrifying. But not as horrifying as slowly sinking in your own muddle of mess. Like quicksand, the more we struggle against life's currents and refuse to be *still*, the more we get pulled down by our *monsters*. But the moment we let go and open our hearts to all that the universe has to offer, life becomes more solid, and we stop sinking.

SURRENDER

When we completely let go and not struggle against it, when we can embrace the groundlessness of our situation and relax into its dynamic quality, that's called enlightenment.
—Pema Chödrön, *Living Beautifully*

O n New Year's Eve, I lay in the tub letting the hot water and wine drag me into in a state of delirium. I had no date. No plans. Nowhere to go. It was just me and *Suffering*.

> *I want to surrender. I want to stop Suffering.*
> *I want to surrender. I want to stop Suffering.*
> *I want to surrender. I want to stop Suffering.*

I spoke the words not out loud, but deep inside as if I was afraid to hear my own voice, as if the truth would incinerate me. For years, I'd told myself that I was going to let go, to trust God. But then some crisis or catastrophe would send me wobbling like a toddler.

For the record, I was a *fixer*. I had a knack for ambushing anything or anyone that needed fixing. Whether it was a man, my daughter, or a disheveled pillow, I fixed it. And now, the thought of being the one that needed the fixing sent me drowning in my misery, desperately trying to hear God speak to me.

> *I want to surrender. I want to stop Suffering.*
> *I want to surrender. I want to stop Suffering.*
> *I want to surrender. I want to stop Suffering.*

I don't recall how long I stayed in that tub; I just remember feeling this huge sense of loss, like I was asking God to shed a piece of me. I cried, drank wine, and cried some more until I pulled myself out of the tub, lay on the sofa, and slept. Just slept, oblivious when the New Year came in.

When I awoke on New Year's morning, I started reading *A Return to Love* by Marianne Williamson. Erica had lent me her copy of the book the last time I'd showed up at her place and was so broken that she encouraged me to read it. I took it home and picked it up a few times but quickly put it back down because I didn't get what love I was supposed to be returning to. But this time when I opened the book, I was intrigued by the words that appeared on the first page as if Marianne Williamson knew that I needed to be encouraged to turn the page.

Be not afraid, but let your world be lit by miracles.
—A Course in Miracles

And I kept turning and turning and turning. Soon I would come to learn that the book was grounded in *A Course in Miracles*, a seminal book published in the seventies that guides readers to their own spiritual transformations. I was awestruck at the notion that I had a choice: *I could shift my perspective from fear to love and ask God for a miracle, or I could stay bound to Suffering.*

In all the times I had prayed, I never thought to ask God for a *miracle.* I'd asked Him to keep my daughter and Promise safe, to heal my broken heart, to make a way with my finances, to bless Saving Promise, and for the strength to do His will. But never had I asked for something as simple as *a miracle*. And for the first time in my life, I didn't commit to some predictable New Year's resolution, nor did I ask for all the things I usually requested. This time I just asked for something profound but simple: a *miracle*.

They say God has a sense of humor. I believe God revealed his sense of humor the morning after New Year's Day when I went to Starbucks, thinking about ways that I could earn an income while I waited for my *miracle*. I'd come up with three options: I could get a job at Walmart, I could bag groceries, or I could teach online as an adjunct professor.

Hmmm . . . let's see—Walmart, bag groceries, or teach? Walmart, bag groceries, or teach?

I chose teach.

Things were rough, but I wasn't quite ready to work at Walmart or bag groceries or even to return to IBM for that matter. Not that I was above any of those options. I just knew that if I had to clock in at some job, I would surely die. Besides which, I was convinced that I needed to do something that wouldn't interfere with the time I devoted to Saving Promise. So off I went to Starbucks to update my résumé and look for an online teaching job. I'd thrown on an old tattered oversized sweatshirt, baggy sweatpants, a knit army cap, my worst glasses, and a pair of hoop earrings that protruded out from under my hat like two big flying saucers.

Earrings.

Ma pierced my ears when I was five years old. I remember sitting in a chair watching Ma sterilize the needle on the stove, cut two broom straws to plug in the holes, then douse a cotton ball in alcohol that she slopped on my earlobes like she was marinating meat. Ma said it wouldn't hurt, but I knew anything pointy and hot had to hurt.

I'd braced myself then the same way I braced myself now, promising that every day I was going to put on a pair of earrings as a symbol to be brave, to remind me how gratifying it would be once I pierced through the pain.

While I waited for my mocha at Starbucks, I watched a man meticulously underline an article entitled: "When Virtue Becomes Vice: Are Your Greatest Strengths Holding You Back?" I don't know if the article intrigued me as much as the way he had painstakingly underlined it. But after coming off an emotional roller coaster and asking God for a *miracle*, I'd promised myself that I was going to be open to any experiences, even a sign that showed up at Starbucks through an article. Then *Lonely* showed up again.

You should say something to him.

No!

Why Not?

Because . . .

But what about the promise you made to yourself yesterday on New Year's morning?

I know. But I didn't come to Starbucks for that. Just let me get my coffee and get back to my work.

You're always working! You said you wanted to change. To get out of your own way.

I know, but . . .

But what?

I need time—to heal, to focus on my work, which is why I came here. Besides, I've written men off.

But you said you wanted to meet new people, make new friends. He could just be a friend.

But that's why my heart is broken, because of—them!

Don't be so dramatic.

I'm not being dramatic. See, there you go again, getting in your own way. Say something!

No!

Why not?

Because he might think I'm interested in him.

Don't be ridiculous!

I'm not being ridiculous.

Then say something. Do it!

You think so?

Yessss!

Okay. Here it goes . . .

"That article must be very interesting." I gestured at the magazine.

"Well, I like to keep the lines straight."

"The title sounds intriguing. What's it about?"

"It's about virtues and vices and how sometimes your greatest strengths can also be your greatest weaknesses."

"That sounds very interesting. I'd be interested in checking it out."

"You should. In fact, it even goes into humility and how once you connect with your vulnerability, you can more easily connect with your strengths and weaknesses. People tell me that humility is one of my strengths, but I'm beginning to wonder if humility is a strength that can become a weakness."

"I believe adversity can lead to your greatest strength. What kind of work do you do?"

"I'm a psychologist."

I almost laughed out loud. A psychologist. *Really, God?!*

He extended his hand. "I'm Reid Walls."

I shook it. "I'm Lydia."

"So, Lydia, what about you? What do you do?"

"I'm an author. I write novels." For some reason, I didn't mention Saving Promise.

"Really? I've never met an author who writes novels. I'd be interested in reading your stuff, although I typically read nonfiction or historical stuff."

"Sure, that would be great. So are you from around here?" I was suddenly curious.

"Yes, I live about ten minutes from here. What about you?"

"Me, too. I live in the historical district right off of Main Street. Are you familiar with the historical district?"

"Yes, but I don't spend a lot of time in the historical district because of parking. Where are you originally from?"

"Well, I've been in this area for about fifteen years, but I'm originally from Philly."

"I'm from Philly too. In fact, my mother still lives right outside of Philly."

"Maybe we can exchange information."

"Sure. I'll go grab my card."

I went back to my seat and hastily emptied my purse, my wallet, my backpack.

Dammit, no cards! What was I thinking when I decided to leave my cards at home?

Lonely jumped in.

Calm down. Just go back over there and ask him for one of his cards.

For the first time, I took notice of what I had on. Suddenly I felt embarrassed. I didn't look fit to be at Starbucks, let alone to strike up a conversation with a stranger.

I stayed there for a few minutes until I got up the nerve to make my way back over to him.

"Do you have an extra card for me to write my information? I don't have any cards with me."

He pulled out another card, and I wrote down my information.

"Maybe we can finish the conversation some time."

I nodded and made my way back to my seat, awed by God's sense of humor.

When the psychologist called the next day and invited me to meet him for coffee, I agreed. This time I showed up in a decent pair of jeans, sweater, and my *flying saucers*. To be honest, I didn't understand why I'd agreed, except that I'd convinced myself that I was going to be open to any *miracles* that God sent my way. But there were so many reasons why I should have just run as fast as I could, but there was also a part of me that was starving to talk to someone—anyone—especially since I hadn't seen Dr. Vicki in months after I had to cancel my health insurance because I could no longer afford it. More than that, it's nothing short of divine intervention if you walk into Starbucks after coming off of an emotional and spiritual roller coaster and you just happen to bump into a psychologist. And when he shared that he had taken some time off from his work for vacation, I broke every cardinal rule and the floodgates flew open.

Usually, when you first meet someone, you hold back a lot of stuff until you decide if the person would make the *cut*. I had no interest in any kind of *cut* with him or any man for that matter, so when he started asking about my life, I couldn't shut up. With Dr. Vicki and Linda from the TM center, my opening up was fueled with unabashed emotion, hurt, and pain. The psychologist made me feel vulnerable, like I was talking to my best friend. We talked so much that we ended up at his place (another cardinal rule broken), and I plopped on his couch, so ingrained and incessant in my sharing. Maybe it was also because he had hundreds of books and videos and music, many of which were about enlightenment and surrendering. He even had *A Course in Miracles*!

For three days straight, we talked. I cried. I laughed. I repented. I argued. I resisted. By that third night, I was so emotionally spent that I found myself apologizing to him.

"No need to apologize. You are a very special woman, and I think what you are doing is commendable. I know things have been hard for you, but you have to embrace the experiences. Everything in life happens for two reasons—to teach us something or to help us grow."

I wiped the tears from my face and looked at him. "You know, even though things have been rough, I now understand that every experience, every loss, every bit of pain has been a gift, a lesson, or a blessing."

The psychologist stared at me. "Wow, did you hear what you just said?"

I looked at him, not really understanding.

"You said: everything in your life has been a gift, a lesson, or a blessing. That's powerful!"

"Wow, did I say that? It sorta just poured out of me."

"Every time something happens in your life, you should ask yourself if it's a gift, a lesson, or a blessing."

In that moment I understood my *miracle*. That I had to let go and learn to embrace every moment as a gift, a lesson, or a blessing; even a chance meeting with a stranger who would become a great mentor and friend.

FIND A WAY

All of us suffer difficulties in our lives. And if you say to yourself "find a way," you'll make it through.

—Diana Nyad

Within days of returning to work after the New Year, I reached out to the CFO of Xerox Services. His daughter, a student at American University, had interned with Saving Promise and introduced us. I was convinced that I needed someone like him to chair the Saving Promise board, and it had been a year since the previous board had quit. It was time to rebuild.

The first time I spoke to the Xerox Services CFO, I told him my story and about the domestic violence crisis that was affecting millions of women and children, and especially young women like his daughter. Then I drew on my corporate experience to articulate the vision for Saving Promise to launch a national prevention call to action and why I needed someone like him to lead the board. After he listened and said he had no experience working with nonprofits, I said *perfect!*

A few weeks later, I went on LinkedIn, handpicked and wrote a personal letter to twelve corporate executives from global companies such as Amazon, Starbucks, Aetna, Johnson & Johnson, L'Oréal, and MasterCard. When they all agreed to a call, I knew that although I had few resources, I had two things going for me: my story and my vision.

Six months and multiple calls and meetings later, I was beyond humbled when they all said *yes*.

There are no words to describe how big that three-letter word made me feel. I knew they had all signed up because they believed in me. And soon they would come to know that they were not just saying yes to Saving Promise, but they were saying yes to save *me*.

I started preparing for the first board meeting when *Worry* showed up. *What if you fail? What if they quit on you too? What if they find out about Broke and Despair and Suffering?*

I freaked out!

Worry was right! It had been seven years since I first launched Saving Promise, and I'd had only marginal success. But I believed in Saving Promise more than ever, and most of all, I believed in a *miracle*. I reached deep into my soul. I wasn't going to let *Worry* or *Broke* or *Despair* or *Suffering* discourage me. Carrying that weight was like dragging around the little secret that I'd carried around like a ball and chain for four decades.

I was six years old, as innocent and pure as the sky is blue. I remember the room, the center one that us girls shared. A bunk bed brushed against the wall, a dresser with three drawers. One for each of us. The boys shared the back room, and Ma's room was in the front. Daddy had just died and Uncle Lionel had come to stay with us.

The room was dark, illuminated slightly by the hall light that cracked through the door. I shared the top bunk with my three-year-old sister Angie, while Eileen, the eldest, slept in the bunk below. I remember his eyes, his face, his crooked and satisfied smile; the way he touched me. I was too afraid to move, too afraid to do anything.

I never told Ma, never told anyone. Just allowed it to simmer in my chest like a bad cold. And now, I wanted to open my heart to every moment, every monster, every miracle.

I was always the kind of person who needed something to inspire me to get to a different state of mind. When I discovered that I was to be a young mother, I'd go sit in the park and watch other young mothers. When I decided that I wanted to be the first in my family to go to college, I started visiting community colleges. When I decided that I wanted to excel in a corporate career, I befriended women who were shattering the glass ceiling. When I decided I wanted to be a poet, I studied other poets like Edgar Allen Poe and Maya Angelou. And when I decided I wanted to learn to play the saxophone, I rented a used one and played it in my living room.

Then I heard Diana Nyad's story—the sixty-four-year-old woman who captivated the world when she finally succeeded in her fifth attempt to swim from Cuba to Florida, over 100 miles for fifty-three hours in open, dangerous, and oftentimes black ocean infested with sharks and swarming poisonous jellyfish. I'm sure there were moments when the pain she endured was so excruciating that she wanted to give up. I remember saying to myself, "If she can do *that* . . . what is it I can*not* do?" Either I could throw it all away, or I could swim.

I chose to swim.

Armed with a new board—including Ann from the public relations firm who by now had agreed to serve as the co-chair;

another $35,000 grant from The Unity Fund for Sustained Change foundation; and an additional $10,000 from the Xerox Foundation—I posted a sticky note on my refrigerator with three single, but powerful, words: *Find a way.*

FAIL FORWARD

If we fail and fail again, we have to get right back up, stronger than we were before. To live in a world worth living in, we have to let challenge inspire us. We have to take risks. Be bold. And let urgency conquer fear. We have to be fearless.
—What It Means To Be Fearless, The Case Foundation

While I was building the board, I reached out to some of the most prominent foundations, corporations, and organizations in the DC region. One of the first meetings I had was with the Case Foundation, founded by AOL cofounder Steve Case and his wife, Jean Case. I was instantly drawn to the Case Foundation, not just because of the exorbitant amount of funds they invested in change makers and transformative organizations, but because of their "Be Fearless" initiative, which said in part: *If we fail and fail again, we have to get right back up, stronger than we were before. To live in a world worth living in, we have to let challenge inspire us. We have to take risks. Be bold. And let urgency conquer fear. We have to be fearless.*

Inspired, I'd reached out to the vice president of marketing and partnerships and left a corny message that said something like: *At the risk of being fearless, I'm hoping you will be open to a meeting with me.* Then I kept calling and emailing and calling until finally she agreed to a meeting.

The night before the meeting, I meditated, prayed, and went to bed early, contemplating what I would say. After much tossing and turning, I finally drifted off and was startled awake by a strange noise and bright illuminating light. Disoriented, I took some time to figure out that the light and the noise was coming from my cell phone that was vibrating on the floor next to my bed. I reflectively reached down to grab it.

"Mom, you gotta help me! Please, Mom, help me! He's trying to kill me!"

Then the phone went dead.

I bolted upright, the bright photo of my daughter still illuminating in my hand. Dazed, my eyes adjusted to the dark room. "Treasure?! Treasure?!"

I quickly hit the speed dial to ring her back. But there was no answer.

I hit it again. No answer.

I hit it again. No answer.

I jumped up and grabbed my landline phone and called 911.

As soon as I heard a voice, I said, "I think my daughter has been attacked by her boyfriend! She said he's trying to kill her! Please, you gotta help her! Please!"

"Ma'am, where's your daughter?"

"She lives in DC." I rattled off her address.

"Ma'am this is the Howard County Police Department. You need to call the DC police. Let me get you their number."

I hung up and quickly dialed the DC police, told them the same thing, and rattled off her address again.

"Ma'am, we're dispatching an officer now. Please stay on the line with me. The officer will be there in a few minutes."

"He's going to kill her! Please, you have to hurry!"

"Ma'am, where are you?"

"I live in Ellicott City. She called me, and I tried calling her back, but there was no answer."

"Do you know her boyfriend?"

"His name is Bobby. That's all I know."

"Okay, ma'am. The officer is at your daughter's apartment. They are going to call you. Please hang up so they can call you."

I hung up, and less than a minute later my phone rang.

"Ma'am, we're at your daughter's apartment complex, but we can't get in because it's a gated community. Do you have a key to the gate?"

"I live in Ellicott City, an hour away!"

"Okay, ma'am. Let me see what we can do. It may take some time."

"There is no time! He may have already killed her! Ya'll gotta get in there now! Please!"

"Okay, ma'am. We'll see what we can do."

I hung up my landline, and then I used my cell phone to call my daughter again. This time she answered.

"Treasure, what's going on? Are you hurt?"

She didn't answer, just cried.

"I know you can't talk. Just say yes or no. Are you hurt?"

"Yes."

"Is he still there?"

"Yes."

"Okay. Can you hand the phone to him; just hand the phone to him, okay?"

Moments passed before I heard the phone go dead.

I dialed her back again, and this time he answered.

"Bobby?! Bobby?!"

"What?!" I could hear my daughter crying in the background.

"Bobby, please don't hurt my daughter! I'm begging you! Please just walk away! Please!"

"She made me do this! I told her to stop playing games with me."

"I know, Bobby, but if you hurt her, you're going to get in a lot of trouble. So, please, just walk away."

"I ain't going nowhere!"

I closed my eyes, trying desperately to think. "Bobby, I don't know if my daughter told you what I do for a living. But if you hurt her, I am going to see to it that you never see the light of day again. Do you understand? So I'm begging you to just walk away and leave her alone!"

The phone went dead again just as my landline rang. It was the officer.

"Ma'am, we can't get through the gate. Is there any way you can call the building management or someone who may have a key?"

"I just spoke to him! He is going to kill her! You have to break that gate open and get in there! Do you understand!"

"Alright, ma'am."

The officer hung up, and I kept calling my daughter, but there was no answer, and every terrible thought crossed my mind. I felt sick.

A few minutes later, my phone rang again. It was the dispatcher.

"Ma'am, the officers are inside. They have him."

"And my daughter? Is she okay?"

"Yes, ma'am."

I quickly hung up the phone and dialed my daughter's cell, and this time she answered.

"Are you okay?"

"Yes, Mom. The police are here, and they have him. I have to go. They want to talk to me."

"Call me back as soon as you're done talking to them."

"Okay, Mom, I will."

For the first time I looked over at the clock. It was just past 4:00 a.m. I waited for her call. About fifteen minutes later, my phone rang.

"Mom, they are going to arrest me! He told them that I attacked him, and they said they are going to lock us both up!"

"What? Where's the officer? Put him on the phone!"

The moment I heard the female officer's voice on the line, I started in, "My daughter said you are going to arrest her! Why are you arresting *her*?"

"Ma'am, because he made a claim that she attacked him first. Therefore, we have to arrest them both until we do a full investigation."

"Are you serious?! This is why victims don't report it! I am a domestic violence advocate, and if you arrest my daughter, I will sue the DC police department and do everything in my power to ensure that you never arrest another victim again! Do you understand?"

"Ma'am, we have to do our investigation. I'm sorry."

When the phone went dead again, I called the police dispatcher back.

"They are arresting my daughter! If they arrest her, I am going to sue the police department! I want to speak to your superior now!"

"Ma'am, please calm down."

"Calm down? This is why victims don't report it!"

"Ma'am, let me see what I can do. I will have someone call you back!"

Desperate, I paced the floor as I thought about who else I could call. Just when I was about to call the domestic violence hotline, the phone rang.

"Mom, it's me. The woman police officer wanted me to call and let you know that they weren't going to arrest me. They had to make it look like they needed to investigate and arrest me too so that he wouldn't get off on a technicality for neglecting his rights."

"*His rights?* He got rights?!"

"I know, Mom, but they encouraged me to go down to the courthouse first thing this morning to press charges and file a restraining order."

"Are you alright? Are you hurt? What happened?"

"Yes, Mom. I'm okay, but I don't want to tell you because you're going to worry, but this time I'm going down to the courthouse to press charges and file a restraining order."

"I'm not going to worry any more than I have already. Please, I need to know, tell me."

There was silence, then I heard her take in her breath.

"When I got home from work around midnight, he had been here waiting up for me and he was angry because he said I left him here all day with no food in the house. Then he called me all kinds of names, and when I ran into the bathroom to get away from him, he followed me in there and started beating me and slamming my head into the tub. When I was finally able to get away from him, I ran into the bedroom, then he followed me in there and started choking me and put the pillow over my head so I couldn't breathe. I tried to fight back, but the more I fought back, the more he beat and choked and smothered me. Then he tried to talk to me, and when I wouldn't listen, he beat and choked and smothered me again. He said he was going to kill me. This went on for hours until I was finally able to get away from him and call you. The police took photos of me and the apartment because there was blood. They even scanned my body with this magnetic thing that could trace the bruises around my neck and head and blood throughout the apartment."

I closed my eyes, felt the tears slide down my face, and thought about Promise. "Where is Promise? Is Promise okay?"

"Promise was at her dad's house. She stayed with him because I had to work tonight."

I stayed silent, still lost for words.

"Mom, I need to change my locks because they took my keys from him, but he may have an extra set and the officer said he could be out within forty-eight hours. They were taking him to the hospital first because he started throwing up and fainted when they said they were going to arrest him."

Fucking coward. That's literally what ran through my mind. *Fucking coward.* There he was beating on my daughter and had the nerve to vomit and faint when they tried to arrest him.

I was angry!

Angry at him. Angry at her. Angry at the system. Angry at me for feeling like I always had to *rescue* her. I was tired of rescuing her! In fact, over the past few months, I hadn't talked to her since Christmas about Bobby and her relationship since she decided to go back to him. Whenever we talked, she would prance around the topic. I could tell she felt lost, but not lost enough to leave.

"You have to do what that officer said and press charges and file the restraining order! I can go to the courthouse with you."

"I will, Mom, but can you just come here and get my locks changed while I go to the courthouse. Maybe you can meet me at the courthouse to pick up my keys and then arrange to have my locks changed."

"Okay." Then I remembered that I had the meeting at the Case Foundation that afternoon and another meeting that I'd scheduled for that morning.

"What time will you be at the courthouse?"

"I'm going to sleep first because I'm really tired, then I'll go to the courthouse later this morning."

I thought about it. My morning meeting was at 11:00 a.m. with Vital Voices—an organization that invests in emerging women leaders around the world who are doing work on violence against women and girls; my meeting with the Case Foundation was later in the afternoon.

"I'll meet you at the courthouse around twelve thirty to pick up the keys."

"Alright, Mom, thanks."

"And, Treasure, this has to stop! You really have to take this serious this time and never let him back in your life again. He could have killed you!"

She got quiet, didn't say anything.

"I gotta go. I'll call you when I'm on my way to the courthouse."

When I hung up the phone, I lay there for a while thinking about everything: the phone call, the illuminating light, the sound of my daughter's terrified voice, the way he had beaten her. For as long as I could remember, I had always turned my cell phone off before I went to bed because I had read somewhere that cell phones emit energy that keeps your mind unsettled. That night was no different. In fact, I remembered turning my phone off, but when my daughter called, the phone was on and lying on the floor, somewhere I would have *never* put it. I *knew* with every fiber in my being that it was nothing short of divine intervention. Had the phone not awakened me, my daughter may have died.

I drew on that divine strength to get up, shower, and dress. I'd called Geraldine, who was scheduled to go to the meeting with me. The moment she heard my voice, she knew something was wrong. Till then, I had kept my personal life *personal*. Not that I was trying to hide anything, but I knew that if I talked about all the things that were happening to me, my daughter, and Promise, I would not have the strength to get out of the bed. But I needed to talk to someone, and that day that *someone* was Geraldine. I told her everything.

There are moments when women band together, and it is nothing short of beautiful.

Geraldine said, "L.Y., you come to my home, and I'll drive us to our first meeting, then we can go to the courthouse to pick up your daughter's keys to get the locks changed. We'll make it in time for the afternoon meeting with the Case Foundation. Don't you worry; we'll get through this together."

Had it not been for Geraldine, I don't know how I would have been able to get through that day.

I felt the hand of God on my life and Ma shepherding me along as I walked into that first meeting with a fixed smile on my face and a heaviness in my heart. Not once did I break stride as I talked about Saving Promise as if my life counted on it, as if my daughter was not at that very moment sitting in some courtroom with bruises on her face and neck.

After the meeting, I felt like I was going to collapse. I made my way to the restroom and sat on the toilet and sobbed with Geraldine in the stall next to mine. Then, we rushed to the courthouse. When my daughter came down to the car to hand over the keys, I felt my heart drop as I looked at the scars, the emptiness in her eyes.

"Are you sure you're okay?"

"Yes, Mom. I'm okay. I'm still waiting for the judge to hear my case. I should be called soon."

"Look at you, you're so beautiful. You don't have to put up with that. You can come and stay with me if you want to take some time away from everything," Geraldine offered.

"Thank you, but I'm fine."

"Then maybe you and Promise can come sometime for dinner or something."

She thanked Geraldine before we left and made our way to her apartment. When we got there and walked in, I gasped. The energy in that place felt dark and dismal. There was furniture and clothes and shoes and food and cigarettes and only God knows what else strewn about. My daughter had been a prisoner in her own home.

"L.Y., we have to clean this place up before the maintenance people get here to change the locks. Let's not let them see that she was forced to live like this."

Every piece of clothing, every shoe, every troubled *thing* that I picked up was like picking up a piece of Treasure. We cleaned up the place in record time, moments before the locksmith arrived.

After he left, we drove back to the courthouse to hand over the new keys to my daughter and then quickly made our way to the next meeting. When we arrived, we sat in the car long enough for me to compose myself before we went inside. Of all the times I'd dreamed about the day that I would walk into the Case Foundation, never once had I'd imagined that I'd walk in with a fixed smile and a broken heart that would soon force me back on my knees.

PLANS TO GIVE YOU HOPE

"For I know the plans I have for you," declares the Lord, "plans to prosper you and not to harm you, plans to give you hope and a future."

—Jeremiah 29:11

Within a few weeks after my daughter filed the restraining order, I sat across from her one Sunday afternoon stunned as she told me that Bobby had moved back in. I could tell that she had lost all sense of herself, felt no more valuable than the bruises that marked her body and spirit.

"How could you?! How could you?! How could you?!" I kept repeating those words, trying desperately to crack through her soul.

I thought about all the times I'd rescued her; the times I'd helped her move; and the jobs I'd helped her get, calling in favors with Saving Promise supporters. I'd even sent her to live with Ma when Promise's father tried to kill her the first time. And when Promise was born, me and Ma banded around her and told her that we were going to be that baby's daddy. We mothered her, inspired her, and told her she was beautiful and smart and powerful.

I'd done all that I knew how to do, and I was done.

Done. Done. Done.

Done with rescuing her. Done with *Worry* waking me up in the wee hours of the night. Done with trying to force her to leave.

There I was blogging, appearing on radio and television, looking into the eyes of abused women at shelters, in churches, on college campuses, telling everybody else what they should be doing while my daughter was involved in one abusive relationship after another.

I felt devastated, ashamed.

All the work I'd done with Dr. Vicki, Linda, Beatriz, and the psychologist, and all the lessons I'd learned escaped me. Now, I looked at her with my heart split wide open. And while I wanted to help her, I also knew that by merely rescuing her every time, I was doing her no more good than Bobby.

When I left her that day, I literally shut down—so down that I became sick for weeks. Most days, I dragged myself out of bed and dropped to my knees.

*"For, I know the plans I have for you," declares the Lord, "plans
to prosper you and not to harm you, plans to give you hope and a
future."*
—*Jeremiah 29:11*

Morning after countless morning, I'd recited that verse. There has to be a *plan*. There must be a *plan*, I kept telling myself.

Months passed.

I marched along like a wind-up doll, going through the motions, like the spirit had been knocked out of me. Especially when I started receiving rejection letter after rejection letter from every foundation, corporation, or individual I'd recently contacted.

Then *Doubt* showed up.

Bombarding my mind all throughout the day and night with all kinds of nonsense. *Why would anyone give you funding when you can't even save your own daughter? Look at you! All that work you did, and you're still in the same place. That's why Purpose and Suffering and Worry are laughing at you. And what would Ma think now?*

I prayed, meditated, read inspiring books from all my favorite spiritual teachers, and watched every episode of *SuperSoul Sunday* and *Lifeclass* on OWN. But *Doubt* was relentless, reminding me why it wouldn't work, couldn't work, that I would fail. Then when the money that John had given me to pay my bills was fast dwindling, *Doubt* conspired with *Worry* and *Fear*. It had gotten so bad that I started rationing food and toilet paper. I'd buy the cheapest food and toilet paper I could find. As if that wasn't bad enough, my car brakes failed and I had no money, no credit, no way to get them fixed. I went to Midas after seeing an ad for $199.

As I sat in the waiting room while they evaluated my car, I looked at a reflection of myself in the glass across from me. I looked terrible. All I saw was *Worry, Fear, Despair,* and *Suffering.*

By the time the mechanic finally came out, I just sat there, slumped, staring at my reflection in the glass.

"So, here's what we got. Not only are your brakes shot, but your rotors need to be replaced and your calibers. You are virtually driving with no brakes. In fact, by law I have to advise you that if you choose to drive with no brakes and God forbid you get in an accident, and harm someone, you can get in a lot of trouble. So for your own safety and the safety of others, I'd suggest you park this car until you can get the brakes repaired."

I closed my eyes to push back the tears. "So are you able to fix them for a hundred ninety-nine dollars?" I knew this was as stupid a question as I looked standing there asking it. But I was desperate.

"Ma'am, the special is just to replace brake pads. You're looking at a minimum of eighteen hundred to get everything done."

"Eighteen hundred? I barely have a hundred ninety-nine, let alone eighteen hundred! Please can we work something out?"

"I may be able to shave off some, but not much. The parts are very expensive to replace. Even if I take off most of the labor, you're still looking at twelve to fifteen hundred. Do you have a credit card that you can use?"

I shook my head and started telling him about *Bankrupt*.

"Well, how about family? Do you have family that could help?"

I thought about John, but I would rather park my car at Midas before I called John and asked for another cent. I shook my head no. "Can you give me a minute to think? I just need some time alone."

When he walked away, I sat there for a long time before I thought to call the psychologist. I hadn't talked to him in a while, but I needed to talk to someone.

"Put the mechanic on the phone," he said after I broke down and told him everything.

I took the phone to the mechanic. A few minutes later, the mechanic handed the phone back to me. "You're all set, ma'am. He's going to take care of it."

"What?! No, wait. Let me speak with him."

I got back on the line with the psychologist and told him that I couldn't allow him to pay for it, then I hung up and went back to the mechanic.

"Are you sure you can't work something out? Please." I started sobbing.

He looked at me. "Ma'am, Midas has a finance program. I know you're bankrupt, but how about I call them and see what they can do."

"It's useless because of the bankruptcy," I sobbed.

"Ma'am, it can't hurt. Let me at least try. Let's have some faith and pray about it, okay?"

I finally nodded and gave him my social security number and license. I felt as broken as my brakes as I tried to pray, mumbling something incoherent. I wasn't even sure what to ask for anymore.

A few minutes later when he came back, I straightened up.

"So I have some good news and some bad news. The good news is there is a God and you've been approved for much more than you need. The bad news is you need to stop being so hard on yourself and learn to trust God."

I started sobbing harder.

There were two lessons I learned that day. One: It was *not* an earrings day; and two, my faith in God, the universe, and the *plan* was restored.

PUT IT IN THE BOX

You have to first accept that what has happened has really happened . . . so that breathing in . . . is like being with it and fully accepting . . . this moment instead of trying to resist it and push it away.

—Oprah Winfrey, *SuperSoul Sunday*

I vividly remember one Sunday morning watching *SuperSoul Sunday*, lapping up every bit of wisdom that poured out of Pema Chödrön's and Oprah's mouths. The force of their words hit me like a bolt of lightning, especially when Oprah said: "*You have to first accept that what has happened has really happened . . . So breathing it in is like being with it and fully accepting this moment instead of trying to resist it and push it away.*" I felt the tears sliding down my face. I could feel my heart squeeze, pulsing through my whole body.

And when Pema said: *Sometimes I say: What does your heart feel like? It feels like a rock. What does your stomach feel like? It feels like a knot. It's as if my whole body was a clenched fence . . .* I started to cry harder. That's *exactly* how I felt—like my stomach was a rusty, balled knot and I was carrying this big rock up a steep hill and every breath I took, every step I made, was like I was sliding back down, grasping at tiny blades of wet grass.

I thought about how much had happened since I had first written that letter to Oprah in 2007, the night that my daughter was nearly killed by Promise's father. I thought about the lunacy of how things unfolded, how much had changed. I imagined what my life would have been like if my daughter and Promise were never born into a life domestic violence, if I had never written *Color Me Butterfly*.

One night I even had this dream where I was floating above a hospital bed looking down at my lifeless body. There I was, my dream self watching me, watch me, as I lie there hooked up to a life support machine. Then I *flatlined.*

I tore from my sleep, screaming, *No! No! No!* Too afraid to close my eyes again, too afraid to die.

The next morning I got up and googled the dream's meaning. It said: *Dreaming that you have died can represent an end of one phase of your life before you enter the next, or some aspect of your life situation coming to an end.*

I knew my life was about to change forever. I was tired of resisting the pain, tired of running away. My moments of misery brought visions of clarity. I thought about the time Promise had stumbled into my office and discovered a Saving Promise brochure on my desk.

"Bumble Bee, is this my name?" She held up the brochure and pointed to it.

"Yes, that's your name."

She pointed to the other word. "So how do you say this word?"

"That word says *saving.*"

"*Saaa—ving,*" she cautiously pronounced.

"Yes *saa-ving.*"

She looked at the two words again and thought about it. "So it says *saa-ving promise?*"

"Yes *saving promise.*"

She tilted her head and a look of confusion came on her small face. Then she said, "But Bumble Bee, what are you trying to save me from?"

Promise was right! Had I forgotten that Saving Promise just wasn't some catchy name inspired by a cute little girl. I lived it *every—single—day*. But the sad truth was that I was scared! Scared for Promise, scared for my daughter, and scared that I would fail.

I took in Promise's innocent face with an identical mole above her lip that she inherited from Ma.

"Ha, Bumble Bee?" She looked at me inquisitively, still waiting.

I didn't know how to put words to a reality that a five-year-old could understand. It's not like when you finally break the news about how babies are made. There are no stories that you can conjure up to explain how her mother's head was slammed into a tub.

Right then I decided to *breathe it in*, accept what had happened, and let go of the pain, the shame, the fears. Because if I didn't, I would not only fail this little girl, but the countless little girls like her, including her mother.

I chuckled nervously and threw up my hands. "I'm trying to save you from me," I cooed as I chased her around the apartment, trying desperately to shield her from the reality that she was born into.

The next day, I bought a beautiful vintage box scrawled in butterflies and flowers and a message that said: *Where there is balance, there is peace.* I'd decided that whenever something ailed me, as Ma used to say, I was going to write it down and *put it in the box.*

My daughter's drama . . . in the box. My bills . . . in the box. People who don't mean me no good . . . in the box. Broken relationships . . . in the box. Secrets . . . in the box. *Despair* . . . in the box. *Worry* . . . in the box. *Fear* . . . in the box. *Lonely* . . . in the box. *Broke* . . . in the box . . . *Suffering* . . . in the box.

I got to the place where if someone said my name wrong, I put it in the box.

That box became my vault for peace.

THE MIND WHISPERER

Enlightenment is the release of suffering—to rid ourselves of negative defeating thoughts, behaviors, and patterns and free ourselves from the habits that bound us.

In Japan, there's an old tradition that when a woman cuts her hair out of volition rather than vanity, it represents her resolve to let go of the *old* and embrace the *new*. It signals a life-altering change. For most of my adult life, I'd always worn my hair short. But once I started putting stuff in my *box*, I'd decided to cut my hair to about an inch, telling myself that I was cutting out all the *drama*.

As I sat in the stylist's chair and watched strands of my hair drop to the floor, I was reminded of my six-year-old pigtails that mashed against my pillow as I lay paralyzed, starring into my uncle's perverted eyes. I could no longer allow all the pain, the anguish of life, to bring me down.

Days after my hair-cutting ceremony, I knew I needed something more than just my *box* and my nearly bald head. I wanted peace, and the only way I would ever have *real* peace was to practice it.

One Tuesday evening, I sat outside the Baltimore Shambhala Meditation Center in my car. The Shambhala teachings believe that *every human being has a fundamental nature of basic goodness* that can be developed through the spiritual path of study and meditation that helps us achieve mindfulness, loving-kindness, and compassion.

I'd arrived thirty minutes early and pulled out my journal to read the entry that I'd written the night before after I'd finished reading a book that I'd chosen to prepare me for the class:

Monday, October 13, 2014

What I hope to gain by reading How to Reach Enlightenment by Polly Campbell is that I will truly embrace the principles and practices to become more enlightened, to allow my spirit to truly break FREE.

To stop allowing my ego and reactive emotions and consciousness run my life. To be more awakened. I pray I can get to a place of unadulterated compassion, connectedness and higher consciousness. I want nothing more than to be at peace with everything in my life.

As I write this journal entry, I pray that I will start on the path of true "uninhibited enlightenment and that I will be "reborn" into a new way of thinking, living and believing. Out with the "old" and in with the "new."

The moment I stepped inside and smelled the healing fragrant incense, peace came over me. There was something special about this place, something that connected with my soul from the moment my toe hit the front door.

A woman sitting at a table near the front door greeted me. "Welcome."

I walked up to her and told her my name.

"We're glad you can join us. There's a place for you to put your shoes over there, and there's tea if you'd like to have some before the class starts. We'll be starting soon." She handed me some materials and pointed out the classroom.

I walked over to the area where shoes lined a shelf, slipped off my shoes, and hung my jacket on a nearby coat hanger before finding my way to the meditation room. Dharma cushions circled the room in front of a red-clothed table with fresh flowers and burning incense that spiraled its scent skyward toward framed images of Sakyong Mipham and Chögyam Trungpa, the lineage of the Shambhala teachings. I took a seat in the circle of other people, mostly *men* (who knew?), then pulled out my journal again and wrote:

October 14, 2014

So, tonight, I start Contentment in Everyday Life. In fact, I am sitting in the class as I write this journal entry. My prayer is that I will commit to not only attend the next five weeks but embrace the learnings and teachings into my everyday life—body, mind and spirit.

I want to let go of the attitudes, behaviors and beliefs that no longer serve me. This includes creating and believing in my "own story"; being reactive when someone says or does something I don't agree with; holding onto ideas, attitudes and beliefs that only fuel the situation; living in the moment and truly embracing the gifts, the lessons and the blessings... because everything truly happens for a reason, even those things that don't feel so good.

I watched the wisdom teacher, whose stature and presence defied his birth age of about sixty that transcended into his spiritual age. This man was everything there is to learn about peace—the way he sat still on the Dharma cushion, his legs crossed, his voice as calm and centered as his spirit, the way he connected with each of us. The minute he chimed the meditation gong, a sound that immediately signaled my mind and body to *rest*, I sat straight up.

He started by telling us about his practice of more than thirty years and then over the next ninety minutes, he taught us about the foundational views of the Buddhist teachings and mindfulness. There is something we all seek, he went on, that's called the Mind Whisperer—to rid ourselves of negative defeating thoughts, behaviors, and patterns and free ourselves from the habits that bound us. We have a choice to accept the moment as it is. It's the art of practicing mindfulness—accepting and being present in every moment, choosing to embrace compassion and loving-kindness toward ourselves and others, and most important, to stop believing in our own *story*.

As I listened to him and others share their stories—from doctors, entrepreneurs, corporate executives, moms, college-aged young people to any number of Janes or Joes—I noticed something so profound: we were all in search of one common thing and one thing only, *peace*.

Every week, I showed up to the Shambhala Center like my life depended on it. During one class—the night that I think that the lightbulb (though already fluorescent), the stars, the moon, and the sun all descended upon me—was when he told us about the Four Noble Truths. These are the Buddha's teachings about suffering: the *truth* of suffering—all that there is, from pain, unease, and change whether mental or physical; the truth of the *cause* of suffering, which is the conjuring up of our own story; the truth of the *end* of suffering, wherein we are no longer hooked; and the *path* of suffering, which cultivates basic goodness. We are often the cause of our own suffering, he explained. Enlightenment is the release of suffering and letting go of our habitual, conventional minds and beliefs, and embracing the basic goodness in ourselves and in others.

Then he went on to talk about Sakyong Mipham Rinpoche, the head of the Shambhala Buddhist lineage and the Shambhala teachings of the Four Dignities—four mythical animals: the tiger, lion, garuda, and dragon.

The tiger, he explained, embraces every moment, slowing down to consider its thoughts, words, and actions and forces us to ask ourselves: "Will this bring joy or pain?" From the tiger grows the discipline of the lion, evolving the mind from the perspective of "me" to the enlightened mind of wisdom and compassion that forces us to contemplate: "How can I serve others?" The discernment of the tiger and the discipline of the lion take us toward the garuda, a mythical bird. No longer attached to the view of "me," the garuda has a 360-degree bird's-eye view, a fresh perspective. Not bound by fear, hope, or suffering, we are freed from the fixation that life will meet our expectations. The culmination of the tiger, lion, and garuda moves us toward the dragon—a deep wisdom that allows us to accept things as they are.

One thing I was certain of was that I was no tiger, no lion, definitely no garuda, and the only dragon I knew was the one that was huffing and puffing the monsters right out of me.

Change is never easy. But at this point, I had spent years meditating; prayed, repented, and prayed again; took guidance from psychologists to wisdom teachers; watched every *SuperSoul Sunday* and *Lifeclass*; languished in the arms of Ma's spirit; cut what little hair I had; and had my mind and spirit broken wide open. I'd come far enough along to know that either I was going to embrace change or change was going to embrace me.

Six weeks later, I sat across from the Shambhala wisdom teacher again in a room much different from the meditation room. I didn't quite know how to describe the experience except to say it's like when you are awakened in a transitional state and you can't move or talk. You want to scream, but you can't. It feels like something terrifying is holding you down. You feel trapped, frozen. You try with all your might to break loose. And just when you are ready to give up and let that force pull you deeper into its darkness, you make one last-ditch effort to BREAK FREE!

That's how I explained my life—my *monsters*—to him. I was almost tearful as I told him that I was just as afraid of finally being *awakened* as I was about being *frozen*.

He looked at me pensively. I had come to appreciate his moments of contemplation—the *Sacred Pause*.

"Did I share with you Raising Windhorse, one of the Shambhala teachings of Warriorship?"

I stilled myself not to reach inside my purse to grab my journal. I had only twenty minutes with him so I didn't want to waste time trying to track down whether this was something he covered in class. I shook my head no.

"Windhorse," he continued, "has a connection with the Chinese tradition Chi—a life force energy that reconnects us with being human. It's the practice of breathing in to feel your energy. By paying attention and being present in every moment, we can raise Windhorse—a deeper ability to connect with the basic goodness in ourselves and the world around us."

Not long ago, I would have thought the whole idea about Windhorse was crap. I could no more *breathe in* to connect with my basic goodness than I could fly to the moon. But there is much to be said about the whole mindfulness thing, and once I started paying attention, I mean really *paying attention*—things changed.

It wasn't easy.

Occasionally, I still struggled with the whole notion that I could just let go of my habitual mind and beliefs. For months,

I just allowed myself to be with *Suffering, Worry, Fear, Despair, Doubt, Broke,* and *Purpose.* And, in time, I felt a paradigm shift. At first, it was subtle like I'd go to sleep each night and wake up a little more enlightened. I once heard Oprah talk about how life whispers to your soul, and when you don't pay attention, it throws you a pebble—a little thump upside the head, and, if you ignore the pebble, life will throw a brick.

I'd had a pebble, a rock, a brick, and a boulder thumped upside my head. If ever there was going to be a time for me to finally *pay attention*, it was going to be now.

It had to be now!

It was time I took a bird's-eye view. It was time I *tiger* up.

TIGER UP

The tiger embraces every moment, slowing down to consider its thoughts, words, and actions and forces us to ask ourselves: Will this bring joy or pain?

Over the next year, there wasn't a day that went by that I didn't *pay attention*. If things were not going my way, I'd ask myself: *What is this here to teach me?* If something didn't feel right, I'd ask: *Will this bring joy or pain?* I'd even gotten to the place where I started cutting loose anything or anybody that had pain attached to it. I won't kid you. I think it was harder to stay present than it was to cling to *Suffering*. Staying present was the most difficult lesson I had to learn, especially when I couldn't find the basic goodness in someone or something stupid. Just because I had become *awakened* didn't mean that the world around me had woken up too.

One of my favorite books, *The Alchemist,* is a tale about how when you want something, God and the universe will conspire to help you achieve it. Let me be very clear. If there is one thing that I know for sure, it's this: once I started *paying attention* to every moment, every meaning, every message, I knew that God, Ma, and the universe were conspiring on my behalf.

But I still had a long way to go, especially with Saving Promise.

So shortly after my meeting with the Shambhala wisdom teacher, I'd consulted the new executive board, and we decided to structure the board into several task forces with two goals in mind: 1) invest our time in areas that could move the dial on domestic violence prevention, and 2) engage relevant stakeholders and funders. At our first board meeting, the chair asked each board member to share why they had joined the board. I was beyond moved when they each expressed how touched they were by my story.

I *could not* let them down. More than ever, I was committed to succeed.

I told the board that I was deeply committed to transforming Saving Promise, and more importantly, the trajectory of domestic violence. But we had our work cut out for us.

While we launched the task forces, I was also promoting my new book *A Life Apart*—the book that I had been writing when I was taking care of Ma. Ann's firm had hosted a National VIP Book Launch Reception that invited DC's socialites, including Congressman Ted Poe. We also used the event to introduce Saving Promise to a host of new stakeholders and funders.

Ann and me at the National Book Launch
To view, visit: lymarlow.com/images

The evening of the event was a blur to me, except for those moments that just stick with me. Like the time I was talking to Kathleen Biden (Vice President Joe Biden's daughter-in-law) and listening to her share how moved she was by my story, then seeing a look of bewilderment come over her face when I suddenly lunged into the story about losing Ma. I'm sure she probably thought: *Poor woman.* But I didn't care what she thought or that she was the vice president's daughter-in-law. It could have been the president himself. I still wanted everyone to know that I did what I did for Ma.

A few months after the book launch, I'd gotten word that The Unity Fund for Sustained Change—the foundation that had given me our first grant for $25K and a second grant for $35K the following year—had just awarded Saving Promise another $75K grant. I was so elated because now I had just enough to build on the board's work and to raise more funds.

Consequently, we'd started planning a summit to invite top leaders from the academic, public, and private sectors, including schools such as Harvard, Stanford, and Johns Hopkins University, to explore their perspective about domestic violence research and prevention strategies. There was no doubt that we needed to collaborate with entities and institutions that had the discipline, talent, and resources to help us. Transforming Saving Promise was not only about operationalizing the organization but tackling one of the most serious public health issues of our time. If we did not believe that we could move the dial on this global crisis, we were doomed.

One of the board members was hosting the summit at Janssen Pharmaceuticals (a Johnson & Johnson company) in Titusville, New Jersey. I felt powerful in my new outfit I'd purchased for the event just the weekend prior.

Within minutes of arriving, a sense of disbelief came over me as I greeted people who not so long ago I'd only dreamed would take my call. I was awed by the caliber of participants and speakers from impressive and wide as the CDC to Harvard. I'd always known that *this* was never just about me and my family story—as I reiterated when I was asked to say a few words to commence the meeting. I'd started by reading an excerpt from *Color Me Butterfly.* I wanted that audience to not only feel the pain that my family had endured, but the pain that countless families endured *every single day.* Besides which, I would only be preaching to the choir if I merely spat stats and talked the proverbial *Houston we got a problem* jargon.

As the summit got underway, I sat in the front row peering up through my readers, literally breathing in every word. I was especially moved when the first speaker, a leader from the CDC opened up his talk with: "Imagine you woke up this morning and you opened up the newspaper and the headline said: Scientists had discovered a new disease that over 50 million women, children, and men were exposed to in the United States, and those people exposed to this disease were at greater risk of mental health disorders, infectious diseases, chronic diseases, and alcohol and drug abuse. What if we had such a disease? . . . Well we do have such a disease. It's intimate partner violence."

To view, visit: lymarlow.com/images

Until then, I'd crafted several strategic plans, hosted brainstorming sessions, done countless press interviews, been invited to speak at high schools to national organizations to peace conferences, and walked the halls of Congress. But nothing could have prepared me for what I had learned that day: *Domestic violence ran deeper than I ever imagined.* Not only were millions of women, men, and children exposed to this type of violence each year, but it also caused all kinds of mental health, infectious, and chronic diseases, including heart disease, diabetes, stroke, cancer, depression, anxiety, sleeping disorders, PTSD (posttraumatic stress disorder), HIV, pregnancy complications, and death. Not to mention the global economic costs were estimated to be trillions of dollars a year.

It was heralding.

Sitting next to our board chair, the Xerox Services CFO, I tried desperately to contain the stream of emotions that flowed through me. Despite all that had come against me and through me, *everything* I had worked so hard for came down to those hours. There are no words for the breadth and depth of my humility and gratitude. And as I stood at the end of a long, intensely draining day sharing closing remarks, the first words out of my mouth were in response to a question someone had asked me: "L.Y., what do you think about the day?" And I replied: "I feel emotionally overwhelmed. *Emotionally overwhelmed.* We learned a lot today—the need to address more evidenced-based research; public education and prevention strategies; a more comprehensive and collective call to action; about the demographic that's most at risk—young people; the economic impact; how do we engage the corporate community and other alliances; how do we influence policy; and, ultimately, where do we go from here?"

I then concluded with the story about when Promise asked: *What are you trying to save me from?* There was an undeniable utter urgency that had escalated with each passing hour and transformed that room into the backdrop of a movement that was just itching to explode.

I wanted to *explode* as I appealed to them to join me in answering Promise's question. It was the day that I knew in my heart of hearts that we were at a crossroads, that now was the time and something *big* was about to happen.

THE ROOTS

There's an old adage that says, "When solving a problem, dig at the roots instead of hacking at the leaves."

I came away from the summit with a laser-beam focus. For weeks, I worked trancelike needling together a plan. Words, thoughts, and visions flooded through me naturally. I was tired of hacking at the leaves; we needed to get to the root of the problem. I was also fed up with the whole *reactive* mindset. In other words, why does my daughter have to be nearly killed before we do something? We needed to think *prevent* instead of *react*. Moreover, it was clear that no one organization could solve this global crisis alone. With this in mind, I'd written a strategic plan that would bring together a consortium of public and private leaders and stakeholders to work collaboratively and collectively. I titled it "*The Partnership to Prevent Intimate Partner Violence*" (which later became the Partnership to Promote Intimate Partner Health) fondly referred to as the Partnership.

I was insistent that we think big, bold, and boisterous, that we distill the naysayers and debunk the status quo. We needed to fight this global public health crisis with as much vigor and vengeance that it had bestowed upon my family and the world.

Within days of finalizing the plan, I scheduled a call to present it to the board member who hosted the summit at Janssen. I knew he would *get it* because not only was he a medical doctor, but he was also the Global Head of Neuroscience at Janssen Research and Development, had previously served in lead positions at the National Institutes of Health, and was the recipient of numerous research and clinical awards. Clearly, he understood the gravity of domestic violence and the impact that the Partnership could make. More than that, I knew he was just the right person to colead the Partnership. He not only had the leadership skills and credentials, but he led with his heart, a heart that spoke to me.

The day of the call, I had thirty minutes to walk him through the vision, demonstrate my own commitment and confidence in the plan, and asked if Janssen would make the first investment to launch it. Our very survival was at stake. If the Partnership didn't work, I didn't know where else to turn. A flurry of nervous energy swept over me. I took my time carefully laying out the plan and pointing out other successful partnership models. I was also mindful not to overpromise, especially given the limited resources and funds.

About fifteen minutes later, I paused to hear his thoughts. Not only did he agree to colead the Partnership, but he also invited me to submit a proposal for funding to Janssen as well as introduce us to other possible partners and funders.

I was ecstatic!

Next, I scheduled a board meeting to share the vision, hosted a webinar to present it to the summit participants, submitted a proposal to Janssen and The Unity Fund for Sustained Change, and launched an advisory committee with a few of the leaders who had attended the summit from Harvard, Johns Hopkins, and the CDC.

I could *literally* feel God, Ma, and the universe directing my every step. Things just began to fall into place—the vision, the connections, the funding. Then something that I'd been praying for for a very long time happened. My daughter called one day and said she had not only gotten rid of Bobby, but she was also planning to move to give her and Promise a fresh start.

I was speechless!

As I held the phone to my ear, I could feel something move through me. It wasn't just relief. Nor was it what I really wanted to say: *About time!* It was what every mother feels when she wants nothing more than to protect her child but can't. No matter how hard she tries, she can't. And she prays. And prays. And prays. Then one day her phone rings, and she hears her daughter's voice on the other end, and she knows that God has heard her.

"I'm really proud of you!" I held back the tears that were beginning to brim. I didn't want to make her feel uncomfortable. "You're beautiful and smart and deserve someone who's going to honor you."

"You're right, Mom, I don't know what I was thinking, but maybe Bobby knocked some sense into me, and everything that happened was for my own good. I'm never going to allow myself to get into another relationship like that again. I don't even like men anymore."

"Don't be so hard on yourself. Not all men are bad. There are good men out there. Just focus on getting yourself together, and in time, the right man will come along who will treat you and Promise well."

While I helped my daughter move into her new apartment, I'd also convinced John to move to Maryland to a new active adult living community that I found only ten minutes away from where I lived. The blunt truth was that it had been five years since Ma died, and it was time that he started to live again. Now that his health was stable, I told him that we needed to sell the house in Lugoff.

"I ain't moving to no Maryland. My home is here."

"I know you and Ma wanted to make a home there, but it's time you stop sitting in that house mourning Ma." In some ways, I felt a little hypocritical.

"Me, you, and Treasure need to raise Promise together. Do it for Ma."

It took some coaxing, but it worked!

Looking back, I had endured *Suffering*, been bullied by *Fear*, had my head filled with *Worry*, confronted *Doubt*, tussled with *Purpose*, been on the brink of *Despair*, been *Broke* wide open, and still carried *Grief* around like she was my best friend—and finally, the miracle that I'd prayed for was starting to happen. Things were materializing for Saving Promise, my daughter was out of that abusive relationship, John was moving closer to me, and for the first time in a very long time, I felt *free*. Like I had shifted into the fullness of my life. But I also knew my life was about to change beyond anything I'd ever known. Something lurking in the deepest corners of my heart, irrevocably whispered to my soul—it's just the beginning.

KEEP MOVING

If you can't fly then run, if you can't run then walk, if you can't walk then crawl, but whatever you do you have to keep moving forward.

—Dr. Martin Luther King, Jr.

The week that I received news that The Unity Fund for Sustained Change was not only going to match the $100,000 contribution that Janssen had contributed but give $105,000, I woke up one day in excruciating pain. Every bone in my body ached.

Soon, I found myself on my doctor's exam table in one of those ugly smocks with my butt exposed, trying to describe the piercing pain that first started in the back of my head and my left knee. (*What the heck my knee got to do with the back of my head, I had no idea.*)

Within months, every muscle and joint in my body ached. I was so fatigued and stiff at times that it was unbearable to get out of bed. On top of that, my body had kicked into menopause to the tenth power, bringing on an onslaught of hot flashes, insomnia, bloating, irregular heartbeats, irritability, mood swings, and night sweats so terrible that I awoke every morning soaked. And if that wasn't bad enough, my cognition and short-term memory was shot.

Most days I'd have just enough energy to crawl out of bed and sit on the sofa with my laptop and phone. I'd be on calls sounding so vibrant only to hang up and crash from exhaustion. For meetings that I couldn't take by phone, I'd load up on Advil to disguise the pain. With each passing day, I could feel my body and mind slipping into darkness. Like I was at the bottom of this deep, dark well looking up at the light.

Several X-rays, MRIs, and blood tests later, I sat once again in the ugly smock waiting for my doctor. I was tired of the probing, the prying, the pain. When I heard the tap on the door and then watched her walk in, I sat impatiently as she explained that the tests were inconclusive and had ruled out rheumatoid arthritis, Lyme disease, and any number of ailments that could cause my pain.

"Are there other tests we can do? The pain is getting worse."

She brought up my records on the computer and stared at it intently. "We've done every test I can think of, and other than a vitamin D deficiency and some inflammation in your knee, your labs are all fine. I know you told me about your work and the stress and then you're also in menopause. Could it be that you're depressed?"

I looked at her like she had two heads. "Doctor, if I were depressed, trust me, you'd know it. I'm not depressed or imagining my pain."

"I'm sure your pain is very real, but I'm not sure how to treat it."

"Then can you refer me to an integrative or holistic doctor? I've tried acupuncture in the past for pain and maybe that can help."

"There is a holistic practice that I've heard about called the Nava Center. A few of my patients told me about them, and it may be worth giving them a call."

Within days I walked into the Nava Health & Vitality Center. Their method was simple. First, they listened. Then they did a detailed assessment, exploring my health, my personal life, and my wellness goals, which was followed by lab diagnostics that would measure sixty-five biochemical markers to get to the root of my pain. By the time I left with a follow-up appointment to return in ten days, I felt like finally somebody was going to be able to tell me how I could go to sleep one day feeling fine and wake up the next feeling like shit.

While I waited for my follow-up appointment, I kicked off the brainstorm sessions with the advisory committee, which were held by conference calls. By now, I could barely walk without pain, so I cut back on any in-person meetings, invitations to speak, and anything that required me to abandon my pink plaid pajamas, which had become my refuge. I was sinking deeper and deeper into the well, mustering just enough energy to crawl out of bed, brush my teeth, and shower. During the first brainstorm call, I sat in my pajamas with the phone pressed against my ear as I led them through fleshing out the Partnership. In hindsight it was laughable. There I was having worked myself into a tizzy over the past eight years praying to be in the company of the caliber of people on the other end of that line, and there I sat in my pajamas, trying desperately to sound normal.

Who the frick knew?

Nobody, that's who! I told no one. Not my family. Not anyone connected to Saving Promise. Not even myself. I refused to be defined by whatever *monster* had invaded my body. I meditated, prayed, lit candles, read, journaled, watched *SuperSoul Sunday*—everything that inspired me. By the time I returned to the Nava Center, I meandered slowly as I followed Dr. Lord, the medical director, into one of the consultation rooms.

Dr. Lord exuded a kindness that immediately made me feel like he was my friend. The moment we sat down, he wanted to know about *me*—asking about my life, where I lived, and my family. When he was ready to discuss my lab results, I felt so at ease that he could have told me that an alien had invaded my body and I would have smiled and said: *Thank you, Dr. Lord.* And it didn't hurt that the man's name was Dr. Lord! *Really, God?*

He started first by walking me through everything that I had shared during my initial assessment about my health, the pain, and my wellness goals. Then he brought up my lab results on a computer monitor that hung on the wall and started explaining how the lab diagnostic test works, the sixty-five biochemical markers and my lab results. When he brought up the page about my hormones with some of the results circled, I was so at ease that it felt like he was talking about someone else.

"Essentially your body is no longer producing estrogen, testosterone, and progesterone, hormones that are very important to your health and vitality. Also, your prolactin levels are abnormally high. In fact, prolactin is usually produced in pregnant lactating women, and when lab results show high prolactin levels, it is usually a sign that there could be a possible pituitary brain tumor present."

What? Did you say I could have a brain tumor?

"Yes, but the good news is that pituitary brain tumors are not malignant and can easily be fixed with medication or surgery."

Until that moment, I literally, and I mean *literally*, had never once given my brain a second thought. I knew I had one. I knew it was this ethereal thing that occupied the space in my head and told me how to think and what to do. But beyond that, it was just one of those things I took for granted until someone told me that something is wrong with it.

The at-ease feeling faded fast.

Although Dr. Lord kept trying to distill my concerns, I was stuck on two words: *brain* and *tumor*. I was no longer in the well. I *was* the well.

"So is the tumor what could be causing my pain?"

"Now that's an interesting question because pituitary tumors don't usually cause any pain, so we still need to get to the bottom of what's causing it. It could be related to the lack of hormones, which we can fix with bioidentical hormone treatments, but I want to refer you back to your primary care doctor to get an MRI and to further assess what else could be causing the pain. But don't you worry, we're going to get to the bottom of this and get you healthy again."

The next day, when I'd made an appointment to see my primary care doctor to get a referral for an MRI, I was disturbed to discover that my health insurance—which was now Medicaid because I could no longer afford health insurance—was cancelled due to a silly form they never mailed to me. I was livid! And, as if in reaction to the news that I may have a brain tumor, I had the biggest headache ever!

There I had been, an abused single mother who grew up in poverty, worked three jobs at times, and went to college at night for sixteen years just so I would never, *ever* have to rely on any kind of public assistance, only to end up bankrupt and on Medicaid. I had never felt so low in my life as I had during those four weeks that I spent on the phone feuding my way through the system to get my health insurance reinstated so I could get the MRI. All the while, I was worried that a tumor could be growing inside my head, not to mention the pain that was incessantly wreaking havoc on my body.

I soon came to learn that any stress or anything toxic sent shock waves of pain through my body that would leave me crippled for days. I couldn't even think bad or stressful thoughts. How *crazy* was it that I'd spent years meditating and seeking spiritual wisdom to help control my thoughts and stress, only to have my body force me to do it. I came to describe it like one of those invisible fences that zaps a pet when he tries to step outside the limits of his boundaries. Every time I tried to go outside the boundaries of my *fence*—which was now my body—I'd get zapped. One zap served as a warning. Two zaps kept me in my pajamas. Three zaps put me in the hospital.

It didn't take me long to learn to respect my *fence*. I'd soon shut down anything or anyone that tempted me to try to cross it. But with each passing day, it was getting harder for me to conceal my illness. I needed to tell someone.

First, I told my assistant, Alli, a brilliant young American University student who had become my eyes, ears, and strength—taking on the lion's share of the work, managing my schedule, even being my memory for things I could no longer recall. I also told Nicole, a savvy attorney turned program manager who worked tirelessly without pay to help me flesh out the Partnership. I confided in them both and asked them not share it with anyone. Not because I was trying to hide my illness, but because I didn't want pity. *Pity* would keep me in my pajamas.

Within a few weeks of telling Alli and Nicole, I was due to meet Ann in New York City to attend a meeting with me at the New York City Mayor's office that had been planned for months. I arrived in New York looking healthier than I felt. It took loads of Advil, energy supplements, and some sensible self-talk to get me off the sofa, out of my pajamas, and on that train. The night before we were scheduled to meet at the mayor's office, I waited at Ann's hotel after I received her text that she was running late. It was well past 9:00 p.m., but I didn't care. I would have waited until morning to see her.

I sat in the dimly lit boutique lobby with its lavish furnishings, thinking about how I was going to tell Ann after being in her company several times over the past few months concealing my illness. Now, all she had to do was take one close look at me and she'd know something was wrong. When Ann finally arrived, I lifted slowly from my seat and followed her to her room. I was grateful for the quiet time and the glass of red wine. After I spent the first forty-five minutes catching her up on Saving Promise, the Partnership, and prepping her for the meeting the next morning at the mayor's office, I felt befuddled as I told her how I woke up months earlier in debilitating pain that progressively got worse and landed me at the Nava Center with an undiagnosed but likely brain tumor. I also told her about being bankrupt and forced to get on Medicaid and that I couldn't get the MRI done until my health insurance was reinstated.

"Since you haven't had the MRI done yet, are you sure it's a brain tumor?"

I thought about the same question that I'd asked myself incessantly for weeks. Whether it was a brain tumor or not, there was one thing that I was certain about: my life as I knew it would *never* be the same.

Ann looked at me compassionately. "L.Y., what can I do to help you?"

It took what little strength I had left to hold back the tears as I told her that it would mean so much to me if she could step in and help me raise funds to hire additional resources so that I could keep Saving Promise moving forward. I also asked that we not share my illness with the board because I didn't want to lose the momentum that we'd worked so hard to build.

The thing that I loved most about Ann was that she was truly one of few women in my life I'd come to admire and appreciate beyond words. As I sat in the backseat of an Uber car that returned me to my hotel, I thanked God for Ann and all the Anns who believed in me and gave me the strength when I had no strength to give.

DEAR BRAIN

It was so surreal, sitting in my pajamas in my living room talking to my brain as though we'd just been introduced. Much like the first time I ever talked to God.

Nearly six weeks after battling to have my health insurance reinstated, I lay inside an MRI scan—a giant coffin-like tube attached to a moveable bed—with my head inside a scary helmet. You'd be surprised what random thoughts run through your mind when you're lying inside a claustrophobic space having your brain scanned.

I thought about Ma and how she must have felt having her body and brain invaded. I thought about John and everything I needed to do to sell the house and move him to Maryland and about my daughter and how proud I was of her for finally getting out of that abusive relationship. I thought about Saving Promise and all the work I needed to do. I thought about my brain. I couldn't help but wonder if *I* was to blame for being inside that *coffin*.

I'd once read that you can change the state of your brain by merely filling it with positive thoughts. So rather than drive myself nuts thinking about whether a tumor was growing inside my head while I was waiting for the MRI test results, I decided to empower my brain back to health. Inspired, I went shopping for the perfect journal. After scaling stores looking for my *Dear Brain* journal, euphoria came over me when I found a beautiful aqua blue soft cover journal entitled: *GREET the day with GRATITUDE, HUMOR and CREATIVITY.*

I'd asked the sales lady to wrap it for me and took it home like a giddy child. That evening, I sat in my pajamas with sweet-scented candles and a hearty fire that brewed inside the fireplace and wrote my first journal entry:

Dear Brain,

Where do I begin? I have so many things I want to say to you. First, hi. I'm pleased to meet you! Funny how in nearly 49 years I have never talked to you and you've been virtually nonexistent until recently when I discovered that you may not be well. I can hardly bring myself to say that five letter word—t-u-m-o-r. In all these years, you've been so good to me—so smart, creative, funny. There have been times when I worked you in overdrive and you never let me down. Always showing up giving me your all. Now it's time for me to take better care of you! Beginning today, I am going to start a new relationship with you by honoring and showing my gratitude in ways that I've not in the past. Here's three things to start:

1) Nurture and nourish you with positive thoughts. I will try my darnedest to not feed you with negative, self-defeating, egotistical or bad thoughts.
2) Refresh and rejuvenate you by allowing you to relax and take time off.
3) Feed you with nutritional things to help you grow and live a healthy and happy life.

With deepest gratitude!

It felt so surreal, sitting in my pajamas in my living room talking to my brain as though we'd just been introduced. Much like the first time I ever talked to God. I knew God was there, but I couldn't see him or touch him. At least not in the way you touch your arm or hug your child. A touch and the hug came in subtle ways—like a gift here, a blessing there. Funny how I now thought about my brain all the time: noticing its every thought, its aches; treating it like a newborn baby by feeding it with nurturing thoughts; ensuring it got plenty of rest; and changing its dirty diapers (in this case, my negative thoughts).

A few days after having the MRI, my doctor called. *Worry* flashed all kinds of dooming thoughts through *Brain*, convincing me that I was about to be told that I was going to die. The doctor was very careful with her words as she read the results right from the report.

Asymmetric fullness of the right pituitary gland,
with no discrete pituitary mass.

"What does that mean?"

"It means that the MRI shows some abnormality, which is consistent with the high prolactin levels, but it appears there is no discrete tumor or mass. I'm going to refer you to a neurologist for further evaluation."

I wanted the test results to relieve *Worry*, but the deterioration of my well-being convinced me that despite what that report said, something was triggering my pain and causing my brain to appear abnormal and produce high levels of prolactin. By now, I had already researched every local doctor that specialized in pituitary brain disorders and learned that there was a Johns Hopkins Pituitary Center in Baltimore, Maryland—part of one of the leading healthcare systems in the United States—which happened to be only forty-five minutes away from my home.

I wrote a letter to the Pituitary Center medical review team, outlining my condition and asked to be seen right away. Days later, I was disappointed to learn that Johns Hopkins didn't take Medicaid.

Over the next few weeks, I researched and wrote letters to several other local doctors and found a neurologist who specialized in pituitary disorders at MedStar Georgetown University Hospital, but the soonest I could get an appointment was in three months.

Three months? Were they serious?

I pleaded to be seen sooner, telling them that I had an MRI that revealed some abnormality in my brain. My pleading and abnormal brain got them to push my appointment up to six weeks. While I waited for my appointment with the neurologist, I got into a routine of just being still for hours, praying and writing in my journal. It was all I could do not to go insane.

Dear Brain,
Every day this week as I asked God to heal you and my
body, mind, and spirit, I couldn't help but ruminate on
moments of my life and how it has transpired in these past

years. Particularly those times, like now, that have forced me to pay attention; to humble myself in gratitude; and to be present to what is happening to me and through me and around me. This holds particularly true when I feel every ounce of painful energy that shoots from the middle of my head, down the back to my shoulders onward to my heart, to the barrels of my toes whenever I allow any level of stress, toxic thoughts or negative behavior to enter me. And it is those moments that I ask myself: What are you here to teach me?

Over the next few months, I found myself going from doctor to doctor—neurologist, endocrinologist, rheumatologist, gynecologist, nutritionist—anybody with an *ist* behind their credentials that could heal me.

It was maddening!

I sat in waiting room after waiting room and lay on exam table after exam table in ugly smock after ugly smock only to be given confusing and conflicting diagnoses. More than that, none of the doctors were talking to each other. I began to feel that I was nothing more than a specimen in a factory of other specimens that were being processed through a dysfunctional system that did just enough to bill my insurance company. I had never been so humiliated and disappointed by our healthcare system. It was then that decided I would take control of my own health and healing. First, I started piecing together what I learned from each doctor and my research. Soon I'd come to understand that I was not just battling one health problem but three:

HORMONAL DEFICIENCIES

A condition that can trigger all kinds of illnesses and diseases.
Essentially, when my body virtually stopped producing
estrogen, testosterone, and progesterone—
all of which are important hormones for ultimate health and vitality—
the lack of hormones triggered all kinds of problems,
including prolactinoma.

PROLACTINOMA

A benign brain tumor or disorder of the pituitary gland that produces
excessive amounts of the hormone prolactin. The pituitary gland is the master
gland, which produces several hormones and controls the function
of a number of other glands throughout the body. With the hormonal deficiencies,
my pituitary gland went berserk, producing high levels prolactin and other ailments
trying to compensate for the lack of estrogen, testosterone, and progesterone.

FIBROMYALGIA

An incurable chronic disease that causes widespread muscle and
joint pain and fatigue as well as other symptoms that was most likely
triggered by years of chronic stress that went into overdrive with the
lack of hormones to counter the stress—
as if my body was a car running at full speed with no oil.

Days after my diagnoses, the endocrinologist prescribed cabergoline—a brain medication to address the prolactinoma; I started bioidentical hormone therapy to elevate and balance my estrogen, testosterone, and progesterone; physical therapy to relieve the chronic muscle and joint pain caused by the fibromyalgia; Pilates to strengthen my muscles; acupuncture to improve my sleep, fatigue, and revitalize my energy flow; yoga to balance my body, mind, and spirit; a cocktail of vitamin and herbal supplements to restore my body; and a nutritional plan that included a semi-vegetarian plant-based diet for overall wellness—all the while continuing to meditate, pray, and journal.

I stood in front of the mirror one day and took a close look at my body, my eyes—thinking about the years of stress, the *monsters*. I wanted to be healthy again, better, more vibrant.

Later, I would also be monitored for an autoimmune disease. I could sense that this illness was here to teach me something; to prepare me for what God and the universe had in mind. I'd told myself that I was going to learn and grow from it. It was to become a defining moment in my life as I began the long journey of healing and learning to GREET each day with GRATITUDE, HUMOR, and CREATIVITY.

SHAKE MY SHIMMY

*For that one hour, twice sometimes three times a week, I was
more vibrant, powerful, and sexy than I'd ever felt.*

With a renewed insight, I got out of my pajamas to get on with my life, but life as I knew it just wasn't the same. I was *different*. As though I had gone to sleep one night and woke up with a big yellow *YIELD* sign plastered across my body. Every morning I willed myself to explore the world in a new way. I'd also cut down my workweek to three days so that I could focus on my healing.

Before my illness, I would have let *Worry* remind me of all the things that would go wrong if I didn't work the eighty hours a week that I'd become accustomed to. But I found it challenging to imagine ever going back to *that* life. No longer was I afraid of *Worry, Fear,* or any other *monster*. For the first time in my life, I felt fearless! Fearless to think bigger, the gall to be bolder. I also knew that I didn't have to push so hard, that I just needed to *pay attention* and allow things to naturally unfold, believing that God was orchestrating everything that was happening in my life.

Ever since I was a little girl, I used to believe that God was this statuesque, white-bearded being sitting on a throne behind some pearly white gates. I'd spent a lifetime joining church after church, reading bible verse after bible verse, trying to understand God. Now I understood that no church, synagogue, mosque, temple, shrine, or any other place of worship could have given me a deeper understanding of God than the lessons I learned over the past years. Gone was my fairytale perception, replaced by an understanding that God is not an individual being. He lives within me and, as long as I continue to stay in touch with that infinite place within, I was going to be fine . . . just fine. What's even more clear is that God used not only people to help guide and shape me, but also nearly *everything*—a book, a speech, a sermon, *SuperSoul Sunday*, a rainbow in the sky. He gave me what I needed when I was ready to receive it.

I'd just started my three-day workweek when I revisited the advisory council's recommendations to launch a Learning Lab—a multiyear, multidisciplinary research and development initiative that would explore how domestic violence prevention strategies could fit within the real world. We also agreed that we needed to collaborate with an academic institution to oversee the research and program development efforts.

Feeling all galled up and fearless, I decided to approach Harvard T.H. Chan School of Public Health for two reasons: 1) they had a large and comprehensive research portfolio with an interest in women's health issues, and 2) one of their Public Health chairs served on the advisory council.

Previously, I would have allowed *Fear* to convince me of all the reasons I would be turned away, laughing at my own stupidity to think that Harvard would allow the likes of Saving Promise into their world. Now, my fearless gall and all the lessons I'd learned had taught me that I'd be stupid not to ask.

After refining the recommendations, I'd requested a call with the Harvard Public Health chair and put together some very compelling talking points. On the day of the call, I sat at my desk suited up because I wanted to feel confident and vibrant. More than that, I simply was not about to blow it. Blowing it was not an option.

The moment I heard her voice on the other end of the line, the words just flowed—as though all the pain, the sacrifices, the *monsters*—everything had come down to that very moment.

This was *my* moment.

I didn't try to bog her down with unnecessary detail. I just laid out the vision and told her that *we* had an opportunity to change domestic violence on a global scale. When I was done, I paused to let her take it all in. Really, to let us both take it in because I felt adrift, like someone else had been doing all the talking for me.

"L.Y., first, I think everything you just laid out makes a lot of sense. I also think launching the Learning Lab at Harvard is a really good idea, and I'm going to recommend it to the dean and my colleagues, and I will get back to you soon with a decision. Please send me an outline of what you presented on this call and anything else you think would help."

After we hung up, so many memories flooded my mind— Ma's last words to me; the day I lay curled in agony because my board had quit on me; the time I walked into the Case Foundation while my daughter at that same moment sat in a courtroom with handprints around her neck; the night Promise said to me, *Bumblebee, just don't look at the monster.*

I had butterflies in my chest! After all the rejection, everything that I had been through, I couldn't stop the tears that streamed down my face with the mere thought of what it would mean to work with Harvard. I sent her the materials that very afternoon.

With the Harvard collaboration looming, I needed to get better!

I was beginning to feel better. I'd also started a Zumba class, something I had always wanted to do but just never made the time for.

The first day I did Zumba, I was instantly in love! I hadn't moved my hips like that since I was in my teens! Women of all shades, shapes, sizes, and backgrounds from their early twenties to eighty were shaking their shimmy. Just being in their presence filled me with an infectious energy. For that one hour—twice, sometimes three times, a week—I was more powerful, vibrant, and sexy than I'd ever felt dancing to Latin music: salsa, merengue, samba, and even hip hop. I'd lose myself in the music, forgetting all about the debilitating pain and the exhaustion I felt at the end of each day.

I was going to shake my shimmy back to health!

MY FEETS IS TIRED,
BUT MY SOUL IS RESTED

Though the journey has been long and I am tired beyond measure, my soul bends toward gratitude.

Years ago, I'd walked into Books-A-Million and bought *A Call to Conscience: The Landmark Speeches of Dr. Martin Luther King, Jr.* It was February 8, 2004, days after I'd watched a Black History Month television special that aired some of Dr. King's most memorable speeches. I knew it was February 8th because I saved the receipt. What I didn't know was that nearly a decade later, this book would get me through some of the darkest moments of my life.

Times when I was having a spiritual crisis, I could almost hear Dr. King's voice prodding me along as I read and reread some of his most poetic and prophetic speeches—"I Have a Dream," "I've Been to the Mountaintop," and the Address at the Conclusion of the Selma to Montgomery March. I'd just sit with that book, holding on to it like a baby holds a bottle, drinking in every ounce of nourishment. Sometimes I'd open the book and read whatever page I landed on, believing those were the words I needed to hear.

I was in the fourth grade when I first heard the "I Have a Dream" speech, too young to truly understand the significance of this magnificent man and the healing he would bring to the world. Every February during Black History Month, we got to learn about Dr. King beyond the occasional teachings from the textbooks or the red bound encyclopedia set that Ma had bought for us. Growing up in poverty, Dr. King was the first person of color with power that I had heard speak so eloquently and with so much conviction. When he spoke, there was an electrified, emotionally charged consciousness that rose up in me and made me believe that *anything* is possible. His mighty cadence and climatic voice spoke to the masses like a church bell that rang out in desolate fields. I remember thinking I wanted to be just like him. I wanted to use my voice to change lives. It was the first time that I started to *dream* beyond my frivolous and paltry yearnings.

Little did I know, decades later God would use my voice in ways that I never imagined. My journey didn't start the day I decided to write *Color Me Butterfly* or the night my daughter lay strangled by Promise's father, nor the day I wrote that letter to Oprah. It started when I sat in my fourth-grade class and started to *dream*.

Much like the first time I read the speech Dr. King made at the conclusion of the march from Selma to Montgomery, one of the most momentous marches in American history. Dr. King led the march after hundreds of black men and women, fighting for the right to vote, were brutally attacked on March 7, 1965, by members of the Alabama State Troopers when they tried to cross a bridge into Selma. A day that went down in history as "Bloody Sunday."

Representative John Lewis—a friend and colleague of Dr. King who led the Bloody Sunday march in Selma—described it best when he wrote in his introduction to this speech: "There was something so peaceful, so holy, so profoundly spiritual about moving feet on the pavement. As we walked with Dr. King, it seemed like the Heavenly Host was walking with us."

Moving feet on pavement. My God! I can almost hear the sweet sound of change rumbling against the asphalt of a mighty shift in history. How could I not find the courage to get up off that floor! It was no coincidence that one Sunday afternoon in February 2004, I walked into a bookstore and purchased a book that I would truly come to cherish. That all of this came full circle is nothing short of a miracle—one that was a long time coming, as Dr. King so eloquently put at the conclusion of the march from Selma to Montgomery:

> *I know you are asking today, How long will it take? . . .*
> *I come to say to you this afternoon, however difficult the*
> *moment, however frustrating the hour, it will not be long*
> *because truth crushed to earth will rise again. How long?*
> *Not long because you shall reap what you sow. . . . How*
> *long? Not long because the arc of the moral universe is*
> *long, but it bends towards justice.*

That's exactly how I felt the day that the Public Health Chair told me that the dean and her colleagues had agreed that Harvard would collaborate with Saving Promise. I cried tears of gratitude as I dropped to my knees and thanked God, Ma, Dr. King, and anyone who gave me hope.

For me, it wasn't about Harvard as much as it was about how deeply and profoundly touched I was for a divinely orchestrated path. As I think back on my life, it's very clear that every step—

the trials, the tribulations, the tests—served as my testimony for a higher purpose. Had it not been for the *monsters* that have shaped, molded, and strengthened me, I would not be the woman I am today.

It was during those tough times that I came to know what I am really made of, who I *really* am. Moreover, I've come to trust God and the universe, allowing every moment to preserve and give me what I need when I need it. Being open to the experience allows for the miracle to effortlessly unfold in all of its magnificence. Without the experience, there wouldn't be a testimony for me to share with the world. I wouldn't be sitting here now with my computer pressed against my lap opening my heart up to you.

While I firmly believe that one does not need to go through the *monsters* that I faced to connect with their divine purpose, I equally believe that *everything* happened as it should. Though the journey had been long and I am tired beyond measure, my soul bends toward gratitude.

Dr. King could not have said it better when he recounted the words of Mother Pollard, a seventy-year-old woman, who, after several weeks of walking during the Montgomery Bus Boycott, was asked if she didn't want to ride. And when she answered, "No," the person said, "Well, aren't you tired?" In her ill-formed but heartfelt virtue and wisdom she replied, *My feets is tired, but my soul is rested.*

FROM HOPE TO HARVARD

Our souls collided in a way that is indescribable. Ma was my hope as I sat still with my eyes closed only blocks away from Harvard.

If I'd known that a dreamy, almond-brown, nine-year-old girl from Wilson Park Projects would someday get to go to Harvard, I would have said what Ma always said to us kids: *God is good all the time.*

That's exactly how I felt the morning I awakened in a hotel room a short walk from the Francis A. Countway Library of Medicine, one of the largest medical libraries in the world, which serves Harvard. I couldn't stop the flutters in my chest that moved through me like a rumbling roar of sheer gratitude. I didn't know whether to cry, pray, meditate, or just be *still.*

I chose to be still. To close my eyes and let grace wash over me. Then something miraculous happened. I found myself sitting on that black Lutgens garden bench surrounded by the lush plants and trees, the cascading water, and Ma sitting next to me. We talked but not in the way that our voices could be heard. Our words came from deep within. There were so many things I wanted to say to her. But there was no need to. She already knew. She'd been there all the time, watching over me, serenading me with unconditional love and adoration. Our souls collided in a way that is indescribable. Ma was my hope as I sat still with my eyes closed only blocks away from Harvard.

And I carried that hope with me as I prepared to meet Ann and our board chair, both of whom had come to Boston to attend the meeting with me. I seemed to float the whole way as we walked to the Countway Library, the depth of my emotions boundless. Every step was like a prophesy—a symbolic ending to a new beginning as I said a few words that can be best summed up by one of my favorite prayers called "Lead Me Out of My Doubts and Fears" by Ted Loder:

Eternal God,
lead me now
  out of the familiar setting
    of my doubts and fears,
  beyond my pride
    and my need to be secure
into a strange and graceful ease
  with my true proportions
  and with yours;
that in boundless silence
  I may grow
    strong enough to endure
      and flexible enough to share
        your grace.

The Francis A. Countway Library of Medicine is all that you would imagine it to be—opulent and stately, holding hundreds of thousands of volumes of medical literature, journal titles, medical history collections, and other resources.

We stopped at the guard desk where we were handed our badges and given instructions to take the elevator to the Allen Room on the fifth floor. I'd been in many elevators over my lifetime, but riding in that elevator was like ascending to new heights.

When we found the Allen Room and were greeted by the Public Health chair and her colleagues, the breadth and depth of what I was feeling was nothing short of sheer jubilation and wonder. I basked in the energy that made me feel like I belonged.

After some heartfelt introductions and remarks from the dean, the Public Health chair turned over the meeting to me to lead. As you can imagine, I was blown away to be leading a meeting at Harvard. But I wasn't nervous. Not one bit. I sat at that table and looked at each face as though I'd stared at those faces a thousand times. Some stoic, others serious, all very cordial.

What ensued will forever be lodged in the deepest corners of my heart. I could feel Ma in that room with me, and I knew that anything that happened from that point on would be nothing short of grace.

I started the meeting by sharing the Saving Promise story, a story that had become as attached to me as my heart. Then we would spend the next four hours fleshing out the details of our collaboration. Later those details would begin to take shape and flight; I would return to Harvard to participate in several conferences, meetings, and planning sessions; we would begin raising funds to launch the Learning Lab and engage additional influencers, stakeholders, and partners; and Saving Promise would be positioned to evolve into one of the most prominent domestic violence prevention and social action movements. But as we sat in the absence of what was to come, I could almost see the future unfolding.

Following the meeting, I stood on the corner waiting for a taxi to take me to the airport as the frigid February Boston air brushed across my face. I would hardly remember the drive to the airport or the long lines nor the tenuous process of walking zombie-like through airport security, disrobing. What comes to mind instead are the final moments I spent at *Vino Volo,* an upscale wine bar, drinking a glass of Pinot Noir as I reflected back on the tapestry of my life. The synchronicity of how fate and grace had to coalesce so wondrously like a carefully threaded quilt. Think about it: Just imagine all the gifts that had to be earned, the lessons that needed to be learned, the blessings that had to be timed, the stars that had to align—all at precisely the right time. Even my *monsters* had threads in the tapestry. Had domestic violence not been a part of my family's legacy, I would have never written *Color Me Butterfly*. Writing that book made me deeply experience the violence perpetrated against four generations of women in my family. And, later, had my daughter not been involved in a terribly abusive relationship that also threatened Promise's life, I would have not been inspired to launch Saving Promise.

On Promise's next birthday, she will be ten years old. Ten years is a *long* time to have the courage to stick with something you believe in. I always knew there was a higher purpose for my life—a spiritual journey that has taught me a sacred lesson: God has a divine purpose for every adversity, challenge, and difficulty that shows up in our lives. He may not create the *monsters*, but sometimes he allows us to go through them to serve his grace.

Today, I truly understand the essence of grace in all of its magnificence. I *know* that God, Ma, and the universe are always with me, and there is no fonder way to symbolize this grace than by sharing the following story.

The week that I was working on the final chapter of this book, the one you're reading now, I had a meeting in Englewood Cliffs, New Jersey—only twenty-five minutes outside of New York City—with a brand development executive at one of the largest global consumer goods companies in the world. This meeting was *big*.

Because I'd gotten to New York's Penn Station two hours ahead of the meeting, I decided to take an Uber across the bridge to Englewood Cliffs to avoid any traffic and ensure I arrived on time. When I got into the Uber car, I asked the driver to find a restaurant closest to the location of the meeting. I figured I'd just have a quick lunch and then walk to the meeting. The driver—a very friendly man wearing fingerless leather gloves, a tan Caribbean shirt, and wide dark-framed glasses—immediately struck up a conversation.

"So what do you do?" he asked in a thick Caribbean accent.

Even though I just wanted to meditate, I naturally started telling him about Saving Promise and the meeting.

"That sounds like important work you're doing. Do you have faith?"

"I don't think I could do what I do without it."

"Do you have a church home?"

"Yes," I said and told him that I occasionally attended St. John's Baptist Church in Maryland.

"So you're of Baptist faith?"

When I responded yes, he told me he was a pastor and lunged into a story about faith and God and *believing*. "You know God is always with us every step of the way. All you have to do is call on him, you know that, right?"

"Yes, I know that. In fact, I called on him many times when I was going through some difficult times, and I believe that God had to strip me bare in order to transform me into the woman I am today."

He looked directly at me through his rearview mirror. "Do you really believe that God stripped you bare?"

I suddenly felt like I'd said something terribly wrong, as if I were standing at heaven's gates and had been asked what my biggest lesson was, and I'd failed. *Failed!* I thought about it some more. "No, actually," I rushed to say. "What I meant was that I believe that there is a purpose for my life and God used whatever I was going through as lessons to strengthen and shape me into who I am today."

"That's it, you got it! And as a pastor, God told me to let you know that you will succeed at everything you're doing and you have nothing to fear but him. Do you understand?"

I stared at his face through the reflection of the rearview mirror. "Yes, I understand," I said, feeling compelled to *pay attention.*

My phone rang just as he pulled up to the closest restaurant that was about a mile up the road, a twenty-five minute walk to the meeting location. I profusely apologized for not having any cash to tip him and thanked him for his words of wisdom.

"You don't need to worry about that. You just remember what I said and do good in your meeting today."

I hopped out of the car, took my call, quickly finished my lunch, then started out on the walk down the summer sun-lined corridor with a slight breeze that radiated from the trees. The walk was peaceful and quiet, except for the ground wave of passing cars that swerved by me as I started to talk to Ma and God.

Wow, I can't believe what that pastor said to me. I am never amazed at how you show up. I know you'll be in that meeting with me today, right? And I can't believe that I'm walking down this road with my luggage. Why didn't I call another Uber? That was so silly of me to walk in this heat. What if I'm all sweaty by the time I get there. Dag snabbit! What was I thinking?! Anyhow, God, I hope this meeting goes well. Wait, didn't that pastor say I should have faith. I do have faith, don't I, God? . . . Oh no! Are those raindrops? No way! It is not about to rain! Shit, I don't have my umbrella! Okay. Okay. Don't panic. It's only another half mile or so, maybe I can make it before the rain comes. Oh no! Oh No! . . . No! No! No!

The rain came steady as I scurried with my roller bag, dodging for cover. But the trees were no match for the downpour that came in droves. I ran like hell, dodging from tree to tree until I reached the parking lot, then scurried to the first door I could find. To my dismay, the door was locked. In fact, all the doors on that side of the building were locked! I stopped, barely able to see, and looked around, realizing that I'd run toward the back of the building near the loading dock. A feeling of anguish came over me as I just stood there in the drenching downpour. Lost, wet, and miserable, I just started to walk until I finally found the front entrance.

When I walked into the lobby, a soaking mess, four guards at the front desk all stared at me—my cute lace bra (the one I'd gotten previously from Target) soaked through my cotton white blouse, my tan linen pants stuck to my wet legs, my perfect hair day now a drenched curly afro, my glasses twisted on my face, dripping rain.

"Do you need some paper towels?" one of the guards asked.

"Ah yaah! And the restroom!"

He handed me a handful of paper towels. "Down the hall, the second door on your left."

I dragged my roller bag into the bathroom and peeled off every stitch of soaking wet clothes. Fortunately, I had brought a pair of jeans and a T-shirt with me. I couldn't believe I had worked so hard to get this meeting, and here I was going to show up in jeans and a T-shirt with a wet fro!

I had fifteen minutes to quickly dry off, change, brush my curly fro, wash my face, touch up my makeup, and try to look somewhat presentable. When I emerged and returned to the desk, the guard who had offered me the paper towels said, "Much better."

"I guess so, but I didn't plan on wearing jeans to this meeting."

"Don't worry. You look great. It'll work out."

I finally told him my name, took a seat, and was astounded to see that the rain had stopped and the sun was as full and bright as ever.

Really, God?

A short while later, when the person I was there to meet showed up in jeans to greet me, I was relieved! I stood quickly to shake his hand. "You're never going to believe what just happened to me." As he warmly welcomed and escorted me to the conference room, I couldn't help but be reminded of some wise words that a three-year-old little girl once said . . . *Bumblebee, just don't look at the monsters.*

the GIFTS. the LESSONS.
the BLESSINGS.

We're living in some scary times! With so much mayhem, madness, and misdeeds, it's no wonder that we are all struggling with *monsters*. Whether you're battling *Regret*, clinging to *Worry*, or consumed by *Fear*, you can rise above it and take back your power! I've been there, and, from time to time, I still struggle. But once I finally got up the courage to *Surrender*, I came to understand that everything, *every* miniscule thing *is* a gift, a lesson, or a blessing. Trust me. I know it isn't easy—all that mumbo-jumbo talk about surrendering. But as corny as it sounds, there *is* something far greater than our own sense of self. And whether you *believe* or not, you owe it to yourself to have faith. So, how do you it? First *breathe*. Then take a moment to meditate on the following:

the GIFTS.

The biggest gift of all, as Beatriz the wisdom teacher once said to me, is to understand that *life is happening FOR you, not to you.*

It wasn't until I was brave enough to surrender—even to those monsters that were beyond my understanding—that I came to appreciate every moment is about discovering who you really are!

the LESSONS.

If there's one lesson that saved me, it's this: changing my perspective changed my life.

I had to accept that every monster I encountered was there to serve a purpose; I had to surrender to what is and let go of what was; and I had to open my heart to all that God and the universe had to offer so that I could shift into the fullness of my life.

the BLESSINGS.

While my life was fraught with some scary monsters, once I learned to accept and embrace ALL that the universe had to offer, there was always a blessing waiting in tow.

Know that some monsters come into your life as a blessing, and some come as a lesson. But whatever comes, learn to greet each day with gratitude, humor, and creativity.

L.Y. Marlow is the founder of MonsteRise®—a movement to help you rise above your monsters to embrace your passion, purpose, and power! To book a workshop, retreat, lecture, or to learn more about the MonsteRise movement, visit lymarlow.com.

ACKNOWLEDGMENTS

I could not do what I do without my *village*. Women whom have ushered, cheered, prayed, and even forced me (and not always in a good way) to be the woman I am today. Some of them you have come to know in this book. Women like Ann. My God, what would I have done had it not been for the Anns? Whether the cardinal Ann, the beautiful spirited woman who gave my vision a voice; or the Anns who gave me hope when I had no hope to give; and even the Anns whose ill intentions forced me to tap into my soul. There is something divine and awe-inspiring that happens when women band together.

To Shana Kelly, the woman whom has been the ink in my pen. Her brilliant and skillful editing has helped me to hone and honor my craft. She was the mastermind behind *A Life Apart* and now *Don't Look at the Monster*—pushing me to rise above the perfunctory and dig deeper.

Everything I am. Everything I do. Everything I believe leads me back to the one woman who has always and will continue to forever be paramount in my life—Ma. There is not a day that goes by that I don't think of her, feel her, believe in her. She *is* the wisdom behind my words and my world.

Finally, I want to give gratitude to the one that is dearest to me of all—God—for always showing up at the oddest and most optimal times; and for believing in me, shaping me, and most of all, entrusting me with the gifts, the lessons, and the blessings.

ABOUT THE AUTHOR

L.Y. Marlow is an award-winning author, sought-after speaker and women's advocate whose life journey took her from a legacy of domestic violence to the opulence of corporate America; and now to a life devoted to empowering others. Her story would be notable enough given her tenacity to shatter the status quo. But it would be her courageous decision to step down from a stellar 20+ year corporate career to write her award-winning *Color Me Butterfly*—the compelling and heart wrenching story behind the national organization she founded Saving Promise—inspired by five generations of mothers and daughters in her family that survived more than sixty years of domestic violence, including her granddaughter, a little girl named Promise. This heartfelt and captivating story moved L.Y. to share her journey of tragedy to triumph in *Don't Look at the Monster*—a testament to the transformative power of discovering her passion, purpose and power.

ALSO BY L.Y. MARLOW

A National Best Books Award Winner

The last thing Eloise Bingham wanted was to leave the comforts of her South Carolina home and family. But at the end of World War II, the young wife follows her husband, Isaac, to Philadelphia—only to experience his sinister and violent temper. Eloise's children—and their children and grandchildren—will face their own trials over the next sixty years: Mattie, who has lived in her mother Eloise's shadow, finds it takes a life-changing tragedy to help her break free; Lydia, Mattie's strong-willed daughter, summons the resolve to rise above the cycle of abuse; and finally, Treasure, Lydia's lively daughter, has the chance to be the first to escape her family's destructive legacy.

It will take unconditional love, old-fashioned family values, faith, and fearless determination—already embedded in each woman's DNA—to triumph over a life plagued with unspeakable pain.

Morris Sullivan joins the navy in 1940 with a love of ships and high hopes. Though he leaves behind his new wife, Agnes, and their baby daughter, he is thrilled to be pursuing his lifelong dream—but things change when he is shipped off to Pearl Harbor when the war begins. When he narrowly survives the 1941 attack thanks to the courage of a black sailor he doesn't know, Morris is determined to seek out the man's family and express his gratitude and respect. On leave, he tracks down the man's sister in his

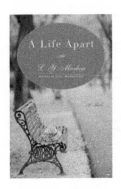

own hometown of Boston—and finds an immediate and undeniable connection with the nurturing yet fiercely independent Beatrice, who has left the stifling South of her upbringing for the more liberal, integrated north.

At once a family epic and a historical drama that brings the streets and neighborhoods of Boston vividly to life from World War II through the Civil Rights era to the present day, *A Life Apart* takes readers along for the emotional journey as Morris and Beatrice's relationship is tested by time, family loyalties, unending guilt, racial tensions, death, and the profound effects of war.

CPSIA information can be obtained
at www.ICGtesting.com
Printed in the USA
FSHW011500040320
67804FS